Man and the Ocean

Man and the Ocean

Brian J. Skinner

Yale University

Karl K. Turekian

Yale University

Prentice-Hall, Inc., Englewood Cliffs, New Jersey

Library of Congress Cataloging in Publication Data

SKINNER, BRIAN J.
  Man and the ocean.

  (Foundations of earth science series)
    1. Marine resources. 2. Marine pollution.
I. Turekian, Karl K., joint author. II. Title.
GC1015.S55   333.9'164   72-13482
ISBN 0-13-550970-X (pbk)
ISBN 0-13-550988-2

FOUNDATIONS OF EARTH SCIENCE SERIES

A. Lee McAlester, Editor

Illustrations by Richard Kassouf

10 9 8 7 6 5 4 3 2 1

PRENTICE-HALL INTERNATIONAL, INC., *London*
PRENTICE-HALL OF AUSTRALIA, PTY. LTD., *Sydney*
PRENTICE-HALL OF CANADA, LTD., *Toronto*
PRENTICE-HALL OF INDIA PRIVATE LIMITED, *New Delhi*
PRENTICE-HALL OF JAPAN, INC., *Tokyo*

Foundations

of Earth Science Series

Elementary Earth Science textbooks have too long reflected mere traditions in teaching rather than the triumphs and uncertainties of present-day science. In geology, the time-honored textbook emphasis on geomorphic processes and descriptive stratigraphy, a pattern begun by James Dwight Dana over a century ago, is increasingly anachronistic in an age of shifting research frontiers and disappearing boundaries between long-established disciplines. At the same time, the extraordinary expansions in exploration of the oceans, atmosphere, and interplanetary space within the past decade have made obsolete the unnatural separation of the "solid Earth" science of geology from the "fluid Earth" sciences of oceanography, meteorology, and planetary astronomy, and have emphasized the need for authorative introductory textbooks in these vigorous subjects.

Stemming from the conviction that beginning students deserve to share in the excitement of modern research, the *Foundations of Earth Science Series* has been planned to provide brief, readable, up-to-date introductions to all aspects of modern Earth science. Each volume has been written by an authority on the subject covered, thus insuring a first-hand treatment seldom found in introductory textbooks. Four of the volumes—*Structure of the Earth, Earth Materials, The Surface of the Earth,* and *Earth Resources*—cover topics traditionally taught in physical geology courses. Four more volumes—*Geologic Time, Ancient Environments, The History of the Earth's Crust,* and *The History of Life*—treat historical topics. The remaining volumes—*Oceans, Man and the Ocean, Atmospheres, Weather,* and *The Solar System*—deal with the "fluid Earth" sciences of oceanography and atmospheric and planetary sciences. Each volume, however, is complete in itself and can be combined with other volumes in any sequence, thus allowing the teacher great flexibility in course arrangement. In addition, these compact and inexpensive volumes can be used individually to supplement and enrich other introductory textbooks.

Contents

Man and the Ocean

1

Man turns to the sea

The earliest remains of man's ancestors are found far from the sea in ancient lake and cave deposits. It is not unreasonable to imagine that the vast, terrifying sea had little to offer prehistoric man. At best it provided a boundary to the seemingly endless terrain he had come to inherit. As mankind evolved during wanderings across the face of the Earth, only two apparently insurmountable barriers blocked the way—the mountains and the sea. The changing sea levels and the changing snow cover of the mountains and plains that resulted from the pulsing ice ages (see Chapter 2) caused wandering man to become isolated from his brothers.

Eventually, when man stood at the dawn of history, he began to build boats and rafts to venture across rivers and lakes. Soon thereafter he took to the sea, and, hugging the shores as much as possible, his boats carried him to remote places.

The great encounter with the sea gave rise to the ancient legends of long wanderings and lost lands. Peoples who had been isolated for thousands of years by the oceans and mountains were reintroduced to each other by the avenues of the sea; thus what was at one time a barrier became the agent for contact at a later time.

Man's early uses of the sea, once he had developed an awareness of its potential as an avenue for transport, were primarily for commerce, conquest, and raiding of unwary sea-protected neighbors. Concurrently, the extension of fishing to the sea from primarily river– and lake–based operations occurred. These primitive uses remain with us today.

With the increasing use of the sea, a need to develop harbors that provided safety in time of storm, as well as bases for commerce, became critical. Whereas the earliest centers of civilization ignored the oceans almost completely and focused at river fordings and caravan routes, these growing maritime activities led to the development of coastal cities with good harbors.

This development in the history of man's encounter with the sea led to many new problems and opportunities. The concentration of people and wealth around such harbors produced a need for more desirable land along the coast, more access to the sea for leisure and pleasurable pursuits, and, finally, a place to discard the municipal and industrial wastes of the growing community.

The coastal communities grew near sheltered and safe harbors, which, typically, have been estuaries, shallow bays, and other protected places. The same sites are commonly areas of high biological activity and are, therefore, naturally abundant larders of readily obtained seafoods. The roots of a now widespread dilemma are immediately apparent. The very conditions that lead to sheltered waters also usually lead to slow dispersal times for debris, and they indicate a system in delicate balance between such opposing forces as silting rates and wave erosion. The sites were chosen for the protection of small communities, but they are rarely able to respond to the pressures of large communities without major offsetting effects being observed in the adjacent marine realm.

Boston Harbor in Massachusetts, for example, was once famous for its vast oyster beds. Farmers of the seventeenth and eighteenth centuries are reported to have driven their hogs onto sandbars exposed at low tide so that they could feed on the abundant oyster beds. But within this century destruction of the natural shoreline, silting, channel dredging, and debris have killed the last of the oysters. The once beneficent harbor life was destroyed by a combination of factors, each probably defendable in its own context as desirable for the good of the community.

The desire for land reclamation is a natural one. Once an established community starts to grow, a combination of land reclamation and dredging of shallow waterfronts to allow the docking of deep-water ships will generally lead to an expansion of living space into the former harbor. Comparison of ancient city maps with modern ones often reveals how extensive this

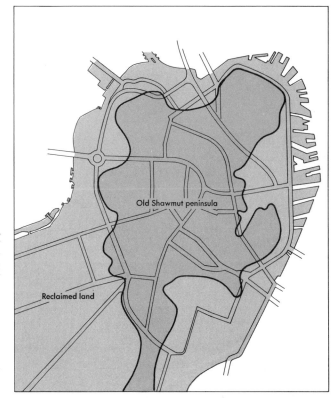

FIGURE 1-1 *Reclaimed land around the old Shawmut Peninsula, a complex of swamps, marshes, and hills on which the Reverend William Blaxton settled in 1625 and which has grown to the modern city of Boston. More than 50 percent of Boston is built on land reclaimed from the sea.*

process has been (Fig. 1–1). In the present century there has been an accelerating movement to fill many shallow mud bays, drain swamps, and, in general, convert shoreline regions distant from city centers to sites useful for mass housing and intensive recreational facilities (Fig. 1–2).

Destruction of the swamps and modification of shorelines with a concomitant disruption of the flora and fauna, as well as any effects that a changed topography may have on aquatic fauna, have produced a growing storm of protest. It is probably incorrect, however, to view all reclamation programs as necessarily harmful or detrimental, and it is easy to identify some spectacularly successful projects.

Nowhere has the process of land reclamation been so effectively pursued, or been so successful in its results, as along the North Sea coasts of England and Holland. The damming and draining of the fens, a great swampy lowland to the north of Cambridge in England, raised storms of protest in the seventeenth century from those who hunted wading birds and fished its waters; but many hundreds of square kilometers of fertile land were re-

FIGURE 1-2 *Land reclamation along the shoreline of major cities continues rapidly. A surveyor checks foundations for a new apartment complex being constructed along the East River shore of Manhattan Island, New York City. Courtesy New York Times.*

claimed as a result, and today the region is one of England's most productive agricultural areas.

The greatest example of land reclamation is in Holland, where 40 percent of the now-inhabited land surface lies below high-tide level and must be protected from the ever-present sea by over 3200 km of dikes, dams, and reinforced dunes. Most of Holland is a large estuarine delta where the rivers Rhine, Meuse, and Scheldt flow into the North Sea. During the glacial ages, when the sea stood at lower levels (see Chapter 2), much of the region that is now the North Sea was exposed dry land. As the sea level rose, the former dry delta lands were flooded and inhabitants were continually forced back. In Holland the fight between inhabitants and the encroaching sea has a long history. The Roman historian Pliny the Elder recorded during his visit to the region in A.D. 47 that the local inhabitants built large mounds in the estuarine swamps on which they protected their houses and livestock from the twice daily flooding at high tide. Commencing in the thirteenth century, systematic land reclamation (Fig. 1–3) has proceeded about equally by the draining of swamps and lakes and by direct accretion along the seacoast.

The direct progeny of such long-standing operations in which man seeks to improve his capacity to use the sea are the many modern efforts to exploit the sea. Continental cables, offshore oil wells, oceanside power plants, extraction systems for chemicals from sea water, and potentially deep-sea

Man turns to the sea

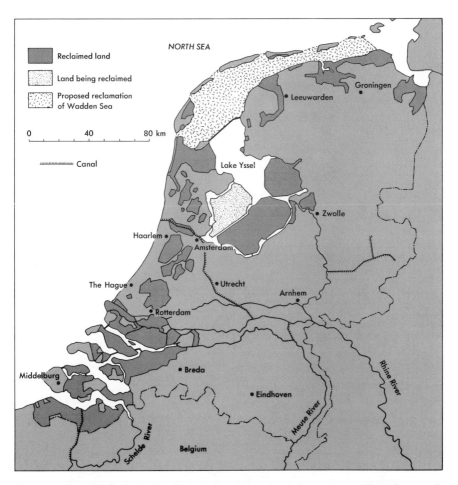

Reclaimed land

Land being reclaimed

Proposed reclamation of Wadden Sea

0   40   80 km

Canal

NORTH SEA

Groningen

Leeuwarden

Lake Yssel

Zwolle

Haarlem

Amsterdam

The Hague

Utrecht

Arnhem

Rotterdam

Middelburg

Breda

Eindhoven

Rhine River

Meuse River

Schelde River

Belgium

FIGURE 1-3 *Much of Holland's productive farmland has been reclaimed from the sea: the dashed area of the Wadden Sea has been proposed for future reclamation. When this has been accomplished, the total recovered land area in Holland will be 7300 km². After N. V. Cartografisch Institut Bootsma, The Hague.*

mining of manganese nodules all share the common feature that they are extensions of man into the sea.

In the following chapters we will describe the status of man's present-day attempts at using the sea. To do so adequately we must first chart the properties of the ocean. The various ways in which man seeks to use the sea for his needs are then described.

2

The oceanic realm

We can think of the ocean-covered portion of our globe as composed of two parts: one is the rocks and sediments making up its boundaries, and the other is the salty water contained in this basin. The two parts are not independent of each other, however. The sediments found on the ocean floor must all pass through the water column, on the one hand, while the perpetually flowing water of the ocean must accommodate itself to the changing topography of the ocean basins. These interactions, together with the air-sea interactions, regulate the patterns of biological productivity, currents, and tides in the oceans, as well as the climates of the continents.

In this chapter we review our present knowledge of the ocean basin and its water in order to show how these findings contribute to solutions of the problems of their use by man.

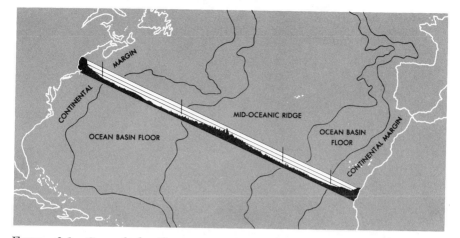

FIGURE 2-1 *General classification of major topographic regions as seen in the North Atlantic. After B. C. Heezen, M. Tharp, and M. Ewing, 1959, Geol. Soc. Amer. Spec., Paper 65.*

The Ocean Basins

As determined from geophysical measurements, the Earth consists of a core surrounded by two clearly distinguishable shells. The boundaries between the three units are called *discontinuities*. The outermost veneer is called the *crust* and is an average of 25 km thick worldwide. However, its thickness under the ocean is significantly less than its thickness under the continents. Using sea level as a marker horizon, the total oceanic crust (including the water in the ocean basins) averages 11 km thick, whereas the continental crust is 40 km thick. The *mantle*, composed of rock-type material, begins at the first major discontinuity in the Earth (going from the outside in), the Mohorovičić discontinuity, and the shell continues to a depth of 2900 km. At this depth another discontinuity is encountered, separating the mantle from the iron-nickel core, which has a radius of 2470 km.

From these dimensions we see that the topographic features of the Earth's crust from the highest mountain (8 km) to the deepest part of the ocean (11 km) involve about 0.3 percent of the Earth's radius. These relatively small fluctuations of the planet's gross dimension, however, occur where miniscule man must live, and therefore we are rightly preoccupied with the details of these planetary wrinkles, which are virtually imperceptible on a cosmic scale.

The topography of the ocean basins can be divided into three major categories: the continental margin, the ocean floor, and the major oceanic ridge systems (Fig. 2–1).

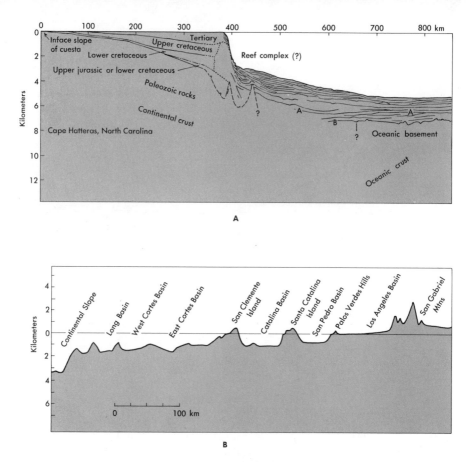

FIGURE 2-2 *A comparison of the continental margins on the eastern and western coasts of the United States. (A) Section from Cape Hatteras, North Carolina, eastward. After K. O. Emery et al., 1970, Bull. Amer. Assoc. Petrol. Geol., v. 54, pp. 44–108. (B) Profile from Southern California to continental slope showing continuation of hill and basin structure from land to the continental slope. After K. O. Emery, 1954, "General geology of the offshore area, Southern California," Geology of Southern California,* Division of Mines, *Bulletin #170, Chapter II, pp. 107–111.*

The Continental Margin

The continental margin varies greatly from one coast to another but generally consists of a *shelf*, a *slope*, and a *rise*. The continental shelf commonly is a submerged extension of the adjacent continent with similar topography and underlying rocks. Thus the eastern North American continental shelf most resembles the submerged equivalent of the coastal plain (Fig. 2–2A), whereas in the western United States the hill and trough topography of that region continues under the ocean surface (Fig. 2–2B).

Where there is a marked change from the gently grading shelf to the steep grade of the continental slope, as exists generally all around the Atlantic Ocean Basin, the feature is called the *shelf break*. The shelf break is located in a water depth of about 100 to 200 meters. A drop in sea level would expose the present shelf, and a rise in sea level would inundate the coastal plain, thereby altering the present limits of the shelf. Such fluctuations have occurred most lately during the ice ages of the last several million years, with the latest event being a rise of about 100 meters in the last 18,000 years.

Incised into the continental slope we commonly find canyons that continue to the great depths of the ocean floor (Fig. 2–3). These canyons have always been under the sea and therefore must have been produced by a submarine erosion process. They represent transportation channels for slurries of sediment and water called *turbidity currents* that not only carve the canyons but also supply sediment and other debris from continental erosion to the deep ocean floor.

At the mouths of many large rivers, a *delta* (Fig. 2–3) is formed on the shelf. Familiar examples are the Rhone, Nile, and Mississippi deltas. As the fast-flowing stream water encounters the ocean, its velocity drops and a mixing with salty sea waters takes place. Both effects cause the suspended stream sediment to settle to the shallow ocean floor.

FIGURE 2-3 *Sedimentary and erosional features on the continental margin. After G. T. Moore and D. O. Asquith, 1971, Bull. Geol. Soc. Amer., v. 82, pp. 2563–2568.*

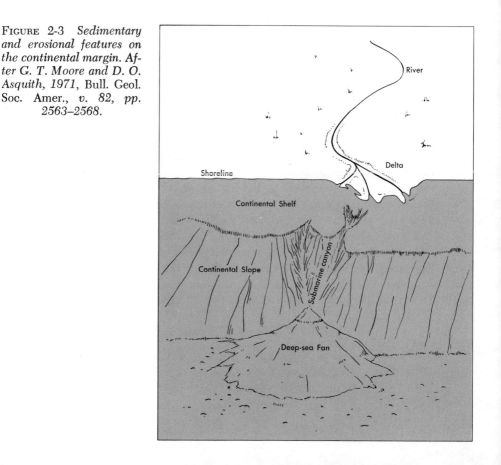

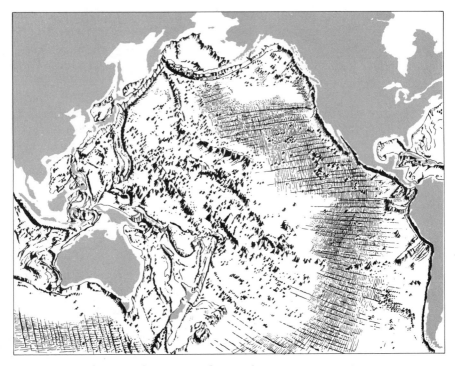

FIGURE 2-4   *Physiographic map of the Pacific Ocean Basin. After B. C. Heezen and M. Tharp, for the National Geographic Society.*

As the delta builds up, slumping of the sediments initially deposited along the outer edge occurs, thereby resulting in the downslope transport of sediment. The material so transported appears as a fan at the front of the continental slope and is one of the features typical of the continental rise (Fig. 2–3). Currents along the boundaries of the ocean basins determine that the ultimate repository of much of this material will be the deep ocean floor.

The continental margins around much of the eastern Pacific Ocean are deep trenches where soundings reveal water depths up to 11,000 meters. The same deep trenches are found east of the major island chains of the Pacific, including Japan and the Philippines (Fig. 2–4).

The Ocean Floor

The deep parts of the oceans, other than these trenches, make up the ocean floor. As a rule, they have a rugged or rolling topography indicative of the action of submarine volcanism and fracturing (Fig. 2–4). Near the continental margins, the continent-derived sediments begin to fill in the rugged bottom features and normally produce a smooth surface called an abyssal plain (Fig. 2–4).

The thickness of sediment underlying the abyssal plains can be as much as 3000 meters. In some areas, such as the Argentine Basin, the sediment pile itself is shaped by fast-moving bottom currents to form mounds (Fig. 2–5).

The Major Oceanic Ridge Systems

Approximately equidistant from the continents on either side of the Atlantic Ocean is a ridge composed of volcanic mountains that rise from the sea floor and, in places, penetrate the ocean surface as islands. Examples are St. Paul's Rock, Gough Island, and Tristan da Cunha. Along the same line lies the volcanic island of Iceland. This predominantly submarine volcanic mountain range is called the Mid-Atlantic Ridge.

A system of world-encircling ridges of similar origin occurs in all the oceans. All are sites of volcanism, of high heat flow, and of relatively shallow earthquakes. The flanks of the ridges grade into the ocean floor and, especially in the Atlantic Ocean, are submerged under the sediments forming the abyssal plains.

FIGURE 2-5 *Physiographic diagram of the Argentine Basin. From B. C. Heezen and M. Tharp, for the Geological Society of America.*

A number of deep basins with long, thin dimensions perpendicular to the axis of the ridge have been discovered. In the Atlantic Ocean, where they have been most thoroughly studied, they appear to be the result of fracturing and differential movement of adjacent parts of the Mid-Atlantic Ridge. Where they are deep enough, these fracture zones may serve to transport sediments from the abyssal plains toward the axis of the ridge. Generally, however, the ridges present enough baffles and "box canyons" to serve as effective barriers and to isolate the deep water and sediments on either side of the ridge from each other.

The Origin of the Structure of Ocean Basins

The major features described above have recently been synthesized into a model of ocean floor evolution that has had broad predictive value. The following is a statement of this model. Other volumes* in this series detail the evidence for it, and they will not be rehearsed exhaustively here.

The surface of the earth is divided into a number of plates (approximately eight), as shown in Fig. 2–6. The plates are perhaps 150 km thick, thicker than the dimension of the crust, and, resting on a "soft" zone in the mantle, can move relative to each other. The major ocean ridge systems are the regions along which the plates are separating; that is, adjacent plates move away from each other along the axis of the ridge. As a result, the "cracks" made by the separation are sites of continuous volcanic activity supplying molten rock from depths that, on solidification, are responsible for the formation of new oceanic crust. Where two plates collide, one plate overrides the other and pushes it down into the mantle, where interactions and melting result in volcanic mountain ranges, such as the Andes (a continental edge plate overriding an oceanic-edged plate because of the rigidity and higher elevation of the large continental blocks) and Japan (two oceanic-edged plates colliding). The deep-sea trenches are the superficial expression of a plane of interaction of buckled-under plate descending into the mantle. The plane itself is demarked by the locus of earthquake foci that extend to depths of 700 km roughly along a 45-degree slope descent under the overriding plate.

The rates of spreading apart of the plates at the axes of the major ridge systems range between 1 and 10 cm per year. Since the buckling-under rate must match the rate of formation of new oceanic crust, it follows that the entire ocean basin must be renewed on a time scale of the order of 150 million years. In conformity with the model, no sediments or rocks older than about 150 million years have been found in the ocean basins.

*See S. P. Clark, *Structure of the Earth*, and K. K. Turekian, *Oceans*.

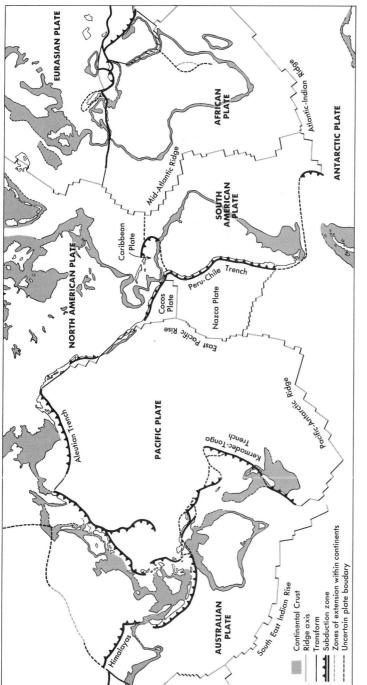

FIGURE 2-6 *The division of the Earth into "plates."*
After J. Dewey, 1972, Scientific American.

The difference between this "plate tectonics" model and the older "continental drift" model lies in the fact that the active units are the plates which may or may not include continents rather than continental blocks themselves.

Sea Water

The Salty Sea

To a very good first approximation, we can think of the oceans as a 3.5-weight-percent (or 35 parts per thousand) salt solution having the composition shown in Table 2–1. The measure of the saltiness of the ocean is called its *salinity*, and the actual range of salinity in the open ocean lies between $32^0/_{00}$ (parts per thousand) and $38^0/_{00}$. These variations are due to loss of water either through evaporation or ice formation, which increases salinity, and to dilution by rain or snow, continental stream runoff, or melting ice—all processes occurring at the surface of the ocean. Figure 2–7 shows the distribution of salinity in the surface waters of the Atlantic Ocean.

The relative proportions of the ions contributing to the ocean's saltiness are very nearly constant despite the variations in salinity itself. Of the major elements dissolved in sea water, only calcium shows a variation of as much as 2 percent when compared, say, to chlorine, and this range is clearly due to the extraction of calcium carbonate by marine organisms to form shells and to the subsequent dissolution of the sinking shells at depth after the death of the organism.

Table 2–1

The Composition of Sea Water*

Component	Grams per Kilogram
Chloride	19.353
Sodium	10.76
Sulfate	2.712
Magnesium	1.294
Calcium	0.413
Potassium	0.387
Bicarbonate	0.142
Bromide	0.067
Strontium	0.008
Boron	0.004
Fluoride	0.001

*Culkin, 1965 in *Chemical Oceanography*, edited by Riley and Skirrow, Academic Press, London.

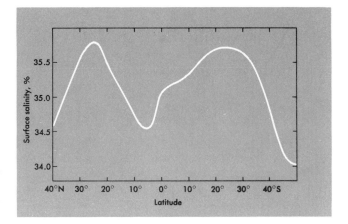

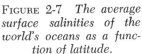

FIGURE 2-7 *The average surface salinities of the world's oceans as a function of latitude.*

Temperature and Pressure

The average depth of the oceans is about 3900 meters. If we exclude the shallow waters of the continental margins and consider only the deep ocean basins, the average depth is closer to 5000 meters. With increasing depth, the pressure increases. The density of sea water is about 1.03 gram/cm^3 (it is 3 percent higher than fresh water because of the dissolved salt), so that every 10-meter-depth interval of sea water equals the mass of the atmosphere and will cause a pressure increase equal to the pressure experienced at the surface. The mass of the atmosphere under the action of the Earth's gravitational field exerts a force. The force per unit area is called *pressure*. The average pressure of the Earth's atmosphere at sea level is called an "atmosphere," so that at 10 meters depth the pressure sensed by a diver would be two "atmospheres." At 5000 meters depth, the pressure, then, is approximately 500 "atmospheres."

The water in the oceanic column is generally warmest at the surface and coldest at the bottom. The surface temperature reflects the local atmospheric temperature as both are heated by the Sun. Heat is also transferred horizontally by displacements due to the ocean current patterns, thus modifying surface ocean temperatures. The deep water below 1000 meters is cold (between 2 to 4°C) because this water forms in the cold regions of the high latitudes. Slow deep-water movements transport this cold water from high latitudes to nearly all parts of the deep ocean; thus even at the Equator, where the surface water is the hottest, the temperature of the deep water is close to that of the high-latitude source.

Stratification of the Oceans

The temperature and salinity of sea water together determines its density. At a given temperature, an increase in salinity results in greater density; and at a given salinity, a decrease in temperature results in greater density. Regardless of how a given water parcel achieves its temperature and salinity, the density determined by these parameters determines the depth it will seek in the oceanic water column. The densest water, formed at the high latitudes mainly as the result of chilling, goes to the bottom.

At the surface, water heated by the Sun forms a *surface layer* or *mixed layer* of constant temperature and density, on the order of 100 meters thick. The lower boundary of this layer is commonly marked by a zone of rapid decrease in temperature and corresponding increase in density, called the *thermocline* (Fig. 2–8). The depth and sharpness of the thermocline vary geographically and seasonally.

The Circulation of the Oceans

The energy of the Sun drives the circulation of the oceans and atmosphere. The surface currents are a direct result of the actions of the wind systems of the Earth (Fig. 2–9). The resulting surface ocean-circulation patterns are *gyre* systems rotating clockwise in the Northern Hemisphere and counterclockwise in the Southern Hemisphere.

The Earth rotates from west to east, so that there is a tendency for the currents to intensify along the western boundaries of the ocean basins. These effects are manifested as the Gulf Stream in the North Atlantic and the Kuroshio Current in the North Pacific. On the eastern margins of ocean basins, surface water is driven away from the coast by interaction with prevailing winds. To compensate for this movement of surface water, an

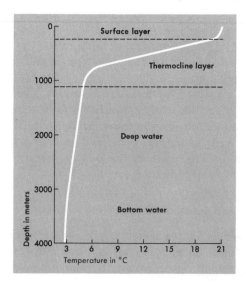

FIGURE 2-8 *A generalized representation of the vertical temperature structure of the oceans.*

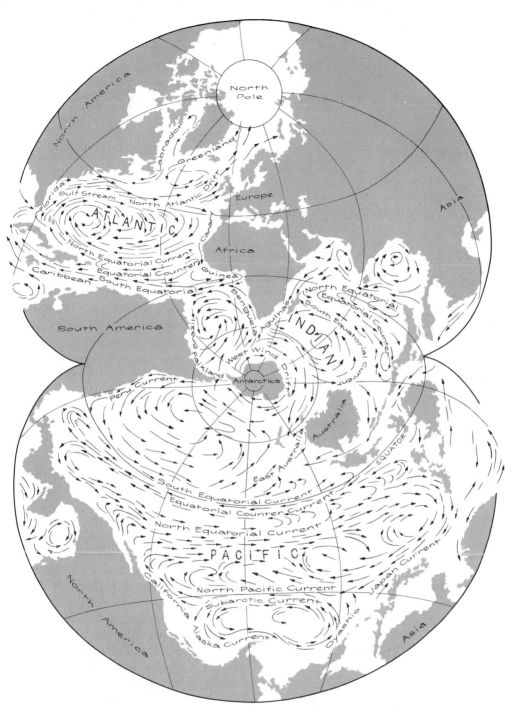

FIGURE 2-9   *The surface currents of the oceans. The pattern of gyres (clockwise in the Northern Hemisphere and counterclockwise in the Southern Hemisphere) can be explained as the result of the major global wind patterns—the prevailing westerlies blowing from west to east at about 40°N and 40°S and the trade winds blowing from east to west just north and south of the Equator. From W. Munk, "The Circulation of the Oceans."* Copyright 1955 by Scientific American, Inc. All rights reserved.

"upwelling" or upward vertical transport of deep water occurs from a maximum depth of 300 to 400 meters. Because deeper waters are richer in the nutrient elements, such as phosphorus and nitrogen, than the biologically depleted surface waters, the arrival of this nutrient-rich water at the illuminated surface zone greatly increases the biological activity of these "upwelling" areas compared to adjacent parts of the ocean surface.

The deep-water circulation is also called *thermohaline* circulation because, as previously implied, it is driven by the dense waters generated at high latitudes that move at depth to fill the ocean basins and then are expended by upward transport.

The surface currents move at relatively rapid rates within ocean basins and probably between ocean basins. Velocities of several knots are commonly observed in the major surface currents in the gyre systems; therefore the surface layer of the oceans can become well mixed in only a few decades. The deep circulation proceeds at a much slower rate, however. Consequently, once a molecule of water is introduced into the deep ocean at the high latitudes, it resides at depth for lengths on the order of several centuries before seeing the surface again.

Estuarine Circulation

Estuarine circulation results from the inflow into a coastal zone of fresh water that is generally supplied by streams. As the water flows away from its point of introduction, it mixes with deeper, saltier water. This process draws the deep water toward the point of mixing to balance the salt water lost by the surface transport away from the point (Fig. 2–10).

As can be seen in Fig. 2–10, a situation can exist in coastal areas where excessive evaporation and occasional chilling cause sinking of water. To compensate for this condition, surface water from the ocean must invade the area. This circulation has sometimes been called an antiestuary.

A classic example, on a large scale, of such a process is the entire Mediterranean Sea. In the Ligurian basin off the French and Italian Rivieras, the gradual evaporation of water during the summers and chilling during the winters result in the formation of salty, cold water that sinks away from the surface. To compensate for the net loss of water from the Mediterranean by evaporation, less-saline surface waters from the North Atlantic flow into the Mediterranean through the Straits of Gibraltar while deeper saltier water flows out. The deep wedge of relatively warm, salty Mediterranean water can be detected at around 1000 meters depth throughout much of the North Atlantic Ocean.

The vertical distribution of nutrient elements (phosphorus, nitrogen, and silicon) in estuaries is markedly different from that in antiestuaries. Carry-

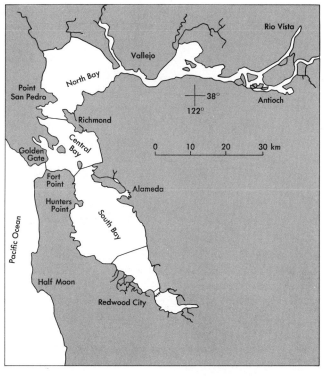

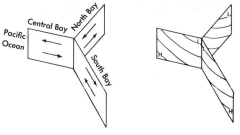

Surface and bottom currents   Salinity gradient

FIGURE 2-10 *Mixing in San Francisco Bay as the result of Sacramento River discharge. The North Bay behaves like an estuary and the South Bay like an antiestuary. After D. S. McCulloch et al., 1970,* U.S. Geol. Surv. Circ. 637.

Maximum Sacramento River discharge. Duration approx. ¼ year

ing on photosynthesis, *phytoplankton* in surface waters extract phosphorus, nitrogen, silicon, and other elements from the water, thereby decreasing their concentrations in solution by locking up these nutrient elements in the plants and animals feeding on them. The particulate debris from surface life, enriched in these elements, is transported downward as the organisms die and sink. Subsequent metabolism by other organisms releases the nutrient elements in solution in the deeper waters, thus increasing their concentrations there. Estuarine waters, therefore, have enhanced nutrient

The oceanic realm

concentrations because of the deeper waters flowing toward the point of injection of fresher water.

In the case of the antiestuary, the vertically transported biological debris, on degradation, releases its nutrients to water that is always being pumped out of the system, and there is no tendency to build up the deep-water nutrient concentration. This depletion means that the return of this deep water to the surface will not greatly enhance the biological productivity, because of the diminished nutrient concentration of the upwelling water. Thus the Mediterranean, a classic antiestuary, is a much less productive sea than the Atlantic.

The Hydrologic Cycle

When we make an inventory of the major water reservoirs of the Earth's surface, it perhaps should not surprise us to find that most of the water is in the oceans. What may be surprising is that the only other major reservoir is in the polar ice caps (Table 2–2). Lakes and streams, and the water vapor in the atmosphere, constitute only a very small portion of the total water reservoir.

This does not mean, of course, that the reservoirs are isolated systems. We know that water is always in flux by way of evaporation, precipitation, and surface runoff as streams. This continuous movement is called the *hydrologic cycle* and is driven by the Sun's heat energy. The most active part

Table 2–2

The Relative Distribution of Water in the Earth's Surface other than in the Oceans

Nonoceanic Reservoirs	Percent of Nonoceanic Water	Volume (km³)
Polar ice and glaciers	75	29×10^6
Ground water at depths less than 2500 feet	11	4.2×10^6
Ground water at depths greater than 2500 feet, but at less than 12,500 feet	13.6	5.3×10^6
Lakes	0.3	120×10^3
Rivers	0.03	12×10^3
Soil moisture	0.06	24×10^3
The atmosphere	0.035	13×10^3
Total nonoceanic reservoirs		39×10^6
Oceanic reservoir		1350×10^6

The oceanic realm

Table 2–3

Water Balance on the Earth's Surface

Process	Units of 10^{20} grams/year
Evaporation from ocean	3.83
Precipitation on ocean	3.47
Evaporation from land	0.63
Precipitation on land	0.99
Runoff from land to sea	0.36

of the cycle is the transport of water from the oceans to continents and the return by surface runoff as rivers. An estimate of the worldwide flux in this cycle is shown in Table 2–3.

Knowing that the volume of the ocean is 1.35×10^{24} cm³ and that the worldwide stream flux is about 0.36×10^{20} cm³ per year, we can calculate that a volume of water equal to the volume of the ocean passes through the ocean every 4×10^4 years. Actually, we cannot determine what happens to each individual molecule of water, so our estimate really tells us that the *average* length of time (the mean residence time) spent by a water molecule in the ocean and associated atmospheric moisture is about 4×10^4 years before it has the experience of being part of a continental stream for a short trip back to the ocean again. Since the oceans are stirred by currents on a time scale considerably shorter than 400 centuries, we can readily understand why the differences in salinity throughout the ocean are really quite small, considering all the processes of evaporation and distribution that locally disturb it.

Water is also transferred from the oceans through the atmosphere to the glacial ice caps in Antarctica and Greenland. The present volume of water stored there is 26×10^6 km³. If this ice were melted and all this water were to return to the oceans, sea level would be raised by about 60 meters, thus jeopardizing the existence of most of the major cities of the world with marine flooding!

The mean residence time of a water molecule in the existing ice caps is about the same length of time as in the ocean reservoir. The loss of water takes place primarily by melting and the formation of icebergs where the glacier encounters the sea. Because ice caps behave like pancake batter, in that they spread under their own weight, their sizes are determined once the edges reach sea level and pieces break off and float away to form icebergs—a process called calving. The sizes of the ice caps on Greenland and Antarctica cannot, as a consequence, be very much larger than they

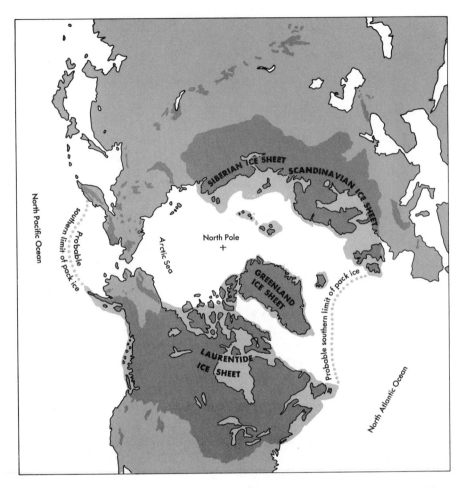

FIGURE 2-11 *The dimensions of ice sheets on the continents of the Northern Hemisphere during the last glacial age. Reconstructed from R. F. Flint, 1971,* Glacial and Quaternary Geology, John Wiley and Sons.

are at present. In the past, however, during the "ice ages," which ended 11,000 years ago, additional ice caps developed on North America and Europe (Fig. 2–11), thereby increasing the amount of water stored in the ice cap reservoir. Since the source of this water is the oceans, its volume correspondingly decreased. The total inventory of ice at the time of the most recent maximum stage of glaciation at 18,000 years ago, for example, showed an increase of an additional 44×10^6 km³. Because of the configuration of the ocean basins, the result was a drop in sea level, relative to the present, of about 100 meters.

This large drop in sea level exposed most of the continental shelf areas of the world. Strandlines, beaches, and other coastal phenomena were all offset seaward (in the present frame of reference). Many of these features have been preserved as submarine relicts by the relatively sudden rise in sea level around 11,000 years ago when the North American and European glaciers melted rapidly.

Another water reservoir with a potentially long mean residence time is found in some of the deep ground water systems of the world. At varying depths below the surface, we always reach a zone where all rock pores and openings are filled with water. The upper surface of this saturated zone is called the *water table*. Where this surface intersects the Earth's surface, it is represented by lakes, rivers, and springs; however, in most places it is below the Earth's surface and may be as deep as several hundred feet. Water below the water table generally moves slowly toward the sea and can be considered analogous to a large and very slow flowing river within which the residence times of water molecules may vary from hours to millions of years, depending on location and hydrostatic head.

Although the volume of ground water is considerably larger than all the rivers of the world (Table 2–2), extraction from this deep reservoir must be done cautiously. A stable, long-term extraction should be no faster than the replenishment rate from rain and snow in order to maintain the volume of the aquifer (as the subsurface reservoir is called). Replenishment rates are low in regions with low rainfall at the present time. Many of these low-rainfall areas, however, have enjoyed higher precipitation rates in the past, and long-lived reservoirs of what is essentially fossil water remain from these times. Their current exploitation in places such as Egypt and Arizona, at rates faster than current regeneration rates, means that the fossil water is being used up and that the subsurface reservoir will eventually become depleted.

When aquifers near the oceans, such as those on islands, are depleted faster than the recharge rate from rain, the danger of saltwater intrusion into the aquifer becomes great. Once this happens, the aquifer must either be abandoned as a source of fresh water until nature gradually reverses the cycle or a massive regeneration program of pumping fresh waste water into the aquifer must be embarked on.

Fortunately, most aquifers occur in regions that are not yet subject to either of the problems just mentioned.

3

The resource concept

Since ancient times the ocean and its boundaries have been used by man for transportation, food, recreation, materials for building and art, and as a source of energy. Such uses continue, but new ones, like communication, mining, production of fresh water by desalination, and waste disposal are being added continually. The oceanic realm has become an increasingly important arena for man's exploitation of nature's resources.

The word *resource*, in the sense used here, means a supply. *Natural resources* are simply those supplies available from the natural environment, such as the food we eat, the air we breathe, and the fuels, mineral products, metals, and water required to sustain our increasingly complex civilization.

Renewable resources such as food and forest products and, in most cases, fresh water, are replenishable because of the direct production of these resources in response to the energy from the Sun, which drives both the photosynthesis process underlying food and forest products and evaporation producing fresh water. (Fig. 3–1). Because the

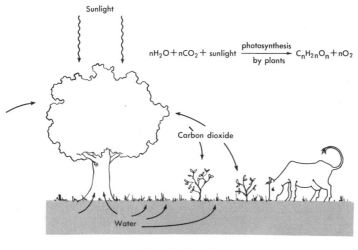

$$nH_2O + nCO_2 + \text{sunlight} \xrightarrow[\text{by plants}]{\text{photosynthesis}} C_nH_{2n}O_n + nO_2$$

A RENEWABLE RESOURCE

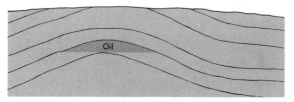

A NON RENEWABLE RESOURCE

FIGURE 3-1 *Renewable resources are replenished through the Sun's energy. One example is the food chain that commences with photosynthesis. Nonrenewable resources are typified by deposits of useful minerals, such as coal, oil, and copper. Although other deposits may form in the future, the replenishment time is so long compared to man's life span that, for all practical purposes, there can be no second crops for the nonrenewable resources.*

storage time of most renewable resources is short, the local limits for their rates of use are most wisely determined by their rates of renewal. Resources like coal and oil, on the other hand, which are drawn from deposits formed on or in the Earth through the geological ages, are not renewed on time scales commensurate with man's life cycle. There can be no second crops for the *nonrenewable resources*; and no matter how slowly we may use a nonrenewable resource, it will eventually be consumed. The size of any deposit is fixed; therefore the continued exploitation of a particular deposit necessarily means that a continuously diminishing amount remains for exploitation—it is then a *depleting resource*.

The significance of the concept of depleting resources can be seen by the fact that our whole civilization, and with it our burgeoning population, has evolved in the context of inexpensively acquired and readily available supplies such as coal, oil, iron, copper, and phosphates from rich deposits undergoing rapid depletion. Although the energy from coal and oil is forever lost once we have burned them, we can argue that such metals as iron and copper, or chemicals like phosphate, are not lost from the Earth after use. This statement, of course, is true and is the philosophy underlying recycling; nevertheless, we find that materials are generally dispersed into progressively less-accessible forms after use. Even where recycling is possible, as in the case of iron, some material is lost by corrosion and other wastes, so that new material must be continuously won from the depleting resources.

Depletion of a given deposit, or group of deposits, does not mean that a given commodity becomes unavailable to man. Because the numbers of ore deposits in the Earth, and their individual sizes, are fixed (though not necessarily known to man), depletion of a relatively rich deposit means that economically less attractive sources must be sought. Local concentrations that have not yet been proven profitable for exploitation but that are still identifiable as possible sources for the future are called *potential resources.*

Renewable Resources: Fisheries

Within the framework of our definition, the renewable resources of the ocean are of three kinds. The most obvious are the living resources of the sea in all their great diversity, used principally for food but also supplying such diverse items as pearls, skins, and whales' teeth. We can also think of the fresh water we extract from the sea as a renewable resource in the sense that ultimately it must make its way back to the oceans after its use by man. This topic is discussed in Chapter 7.

Less obvious and somewhat less tangible is the use of the ocean as a site for the dumping of man-generated waste on the assumption that the quality of the marine environment is maintained by internal processes that degrade and assimilate the wastes. In a sense, then, the capacity of the ocean to accommodate waste without deterioration lets us describe this ability as a renewable resource. The waste-elimination capacity of the oceans as a renewable resource is discussed at length in Chapter 8.

The remaining part of this section will deal with the first named of these three renewable resources—food from the sea.

Food from the sea has long been an important supplement to man's diet in maritime lands. Fish, marine mammals, and shellfish have each been utilized in communities all over the world throughout man's history. Except for the Eskimos, who for thousands of years have hunted marine mammals virtually as their exclusive food source, most communities utilize the sea products, principally fin fish and shellfish, primarily as a source for protein.

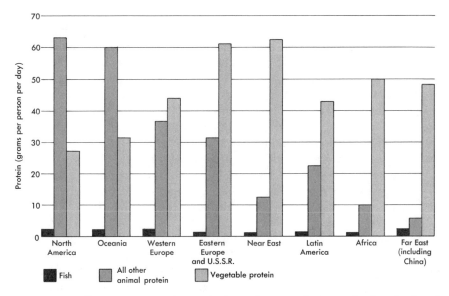

FIGURE 3-2 *The importance of protein from the sea relative to land animal and vegetable protein. After J. J. Holt, 1969,* Scientific American.

Classically, most cultures have met the daily needs for highly efficient body fuel by the use of carbohydrates from agricultural products. At present, on a worldwide basis, the major source of protein is found not in the sea but on land, as is indicated in Fig. 3–2.

The question arises as to whether we can so improve the efficiency of fishing as actually to make the sea an important consideration in solving the Earth's future food needs. The answer to this question, unfortunately, is that normal fishing in the open sea is already near the maximum efficiency consistent with maintaining a viable standing population that can continuously produce harvestable food.

In 1968 the total live weight of animals harvested from the sea was 64 million tons. Of this amount, half was used directly as food and the other half was processed into various forms of livestock feed, including a product called fish protein concentrate (FPC). In the United States most of the fish utilized for food goes to chickens and hogs fed on marine-originated livestock feed. Many fishery scientists believe that the total sustainable yield of food from the sea is about 200 million tons a year. Any more aggressive fishing might deplete the stocks sufficiently that the rate of production of new offspring, and hence future yields, is decreased radically. This situation has already happened in the case of whales. Several species have been hunted so efficiently in recent years by fishermen of several countries that they are now close to extinction and can no longer be considered as dependable resources for continuous harvesting in the future. For this reason, food from the sea may well be limited by biological considerations before it is limited by technological constraints or more efficient hunting methods.

One prospect for extracting more food from the sea without harmful irreversible consequences exists—the systematically controlled farming of the sea. This is, in essence, the act of controlling the crop and monitoring and managing its productivity directly by constant husbandry. The term for this type of controlled operation is *aquaculture* or *mariculture*, as compared to the closest equivalent land-based activity we call *agriculture*.

Today mariculture is used to produce shellfish and fin fish that bring premium prices on the market. In that sense, it is used primarily as a revenue source rather than as a source for the supply of protein for the world's needs.

Approximately 5 percent of the total world catch of sea animals is produced under some degree of control by man at the present time. This control ranges from the most elementary form of manipulation—the transplantation of species from one natural environment to a better natural environment for rapid growth—to the construction of enclosures where the flow of feed for the growth of the desired species is controlled.

Oysters, cockles, and mussels to some degree are now subject to man's intervention for the sake of an improved yield. Completely controlled systems exist for the growth of shrimp in Japan. In this case, scrap fish is used to feed the shrimp, which are then sold as a high-priced gourmet item.

If we seek to extend the process of mariculture in order to provide the protein needs of mankind, we must consider the costs as compared to other sources of protein. Fish low in the food chain, such as anchovies and sardines, cost from $15 to $30 a ton, whereas tuna (as well as chicken) is about ten times more expensive. Mariculture products cost about the same as tuna and chicken. Although, in the United States and Europe, chicken hardly qualifies as an expensive food item compared to other items on the shopping list, such is not the case for much of the rest of the world. Clearly, unless mariculture products can be made to compete in cost with the low-cost hunted species, they will belong in the category of specialty foods, much as chicken and tuna are now.

Ideally, by improved techniques and management, as well as the availability of suitable coastal sites for mariculture, it may be possible to increase yields significantly while, at the same time, keeping costs down. Unfortunately, the coastal zone is also the most heavily trafficked and polluted, a fact that strongly restrains the development of large-scale mariculture. It has been argued that a suitably managed area the size of Long Island Sound could, theoretically, produce mussel meat each year equal to the estimated maximum total annual worldwide fish catch if all other activities in the area were subordinated to mariculture effort.

Nonrenewable Resources

The nonrenewable resources are primarily the *mineral resources,* by which we mean all the nonliving, naturally occurring substances that are useful to man, whether of inorganic or organic origin. Mineral resources are most conveniently classified on the basis of use (Fig. 3–3). The *metallic mineral resources* may be divided into the geochemically *abundant metals,* such as iron and aluminum, which are present in the Earth's crust in concentration greater than 0.01 percent, and the geochemically *scarce metals,* such as copper, lead, zinc, and mercury, whose average crustal concentrations are less than 0.01 percent. Of course, the abundances of metals in ocean water do not follow the crustal abundances. For example, because of the low solubilities of iron and aluminum salts in sea water, their concentrations are as low as the concentrations of copper and zinc.

The Value and Quantity of Nonrenewable Resources Produced

Mineral resources must all be searched for, removed, and processed prior

FIGURE 3-3 *Classification of mineral resources. After B. J. Skinner, 1969,* Earth Resources. *Prentice-Hall.*

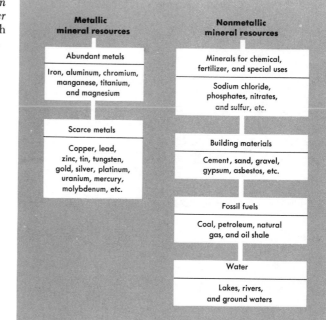

Metallic mineral resources	Nonmetallic mineral resources
Abundant metals	Minerals for chemical, fertilizer, and special uses
Iron, aluminum, chromium, manganese, titanium, and magnesium	Sodium chloride, phosphates, nitrates, and sulfur, etc.
Scarce metals	Building materials
Copper, lead, zinc, tin, tungsten, gold, silver, platinum, uranium, mercury, molybdenum, etc.	Cement, sand, gravel, gypsum, asbestos, etc.
	Fossil fuels
	Coal, petroleum, natural gas, and oil shale
	Water
	Lakes, rivers, and ground waters

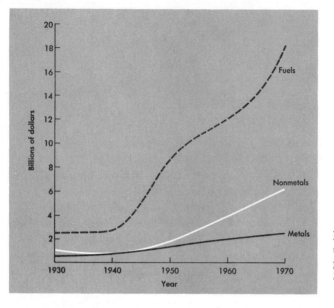

FIGURE 3-4 *Relative value of mineral resources produced in the United States. After U.S. Bureau of Mines.*

to use, and only after these steps have been taken can a value be assigned to the product. The United States is a major producer and consumer of most mineral resources; thus production values for its resources are a good indication of relative values for production of the same commodities on a global scale (Fig. 3–4).

In terms of total production in 1972, the most valuable resources are fuels: coal, oil, and natural gas, amounting to 65 percent in value of the annual mineral production. Despite this high production figure, the United States does not satisfy its needs from internal production and fuels are one of the main imports in the area of mineral resources. Surprisingly, it is not the metallic mineral resources that follow fuels in value but the less–glamorous nonmetallics used for building materials, such as sand, gravel, and crushed rock, plus the chemical and fertilizer materials; these items account for 23 percent of the annual production. Finally, the metallic minerals, which most people naturally think of when mineral production is mentioned, account for the remaining 12 percent. Although the relative values of these three major mineral groups have varied little during the last half century, their absolute values have risen dramatically, both in the United States and in all other major countries of the world. The reason for the increasing value of mineral production is principally an increasing population; however, an increasing annual per capita consumption as living standards rise also plays a part.

The total cash value of mineral production is informative, but it does not tell us how much of a given commodity is produced. We are dealing with depleting resources, however, so the annual production rate is vitally important in any assessments we may wish to make of the adequacy of current resources and of the possible future uses of potential resources.

The detailed discussion of the production rates of fossil fuels, so intimately related to man's future exploitation of the oceans, is presented in Chapter 5, while the recovery of fresh water from the sea is treated in Chapter 6. For the remaining mineral commodities, we can usually assess the world production rates from data published annually by the U.S. Bureau of Mines in the *Minerals Yearbook* (Table 3–1).

Table 3–1

World Production of Selected Mineral Resources in 1971 (estimated by U.S. Bureau of Mines)

Metallic Mineral Resources	Thousands of Metric Tons
Aluminum	10,020
Chromium ore	5,995
Cobalt	20
Copper	5,880
Gold	1.5
Ilmenite	3,399
Lead	3,323
Magnesium	226
Manganese oxide	19,064
Mercury	9.6
Molybdenum[a]	70
Nickel	643
Platinum	0.12
Rutile[a]	391
Silver	9.5
Steel	578,000
Thorium[a]	0.7
Tin	233
Tungsten	32
Uranium[a]	22
Zinc	5,416

Nonmetallic Resources	Thousands of Metric Tons
Bromine	14
Cement	605,000
Gypsum	51,549
Limestone	98,908
Phosphorite	83,638
Potash (as K_2O)	18,700
Salt	143,068
Sand and gravel	5,449,990
Stone (crushed)[a]	4,004,000
Sulfur	38,402

[a]Does not include production from Communist countries.

The resource concept

General Rules Governing Exploitation of Nonrenewable Resources

The cardinal rule governing the production of all mineral resources is that the costs of discovery plus recovery be no greater than the value of the material on the competitive world market. Behind this simple statement are several interacting variables. The most important limiting variable is the grade, which simply means the richness or percentage of the desired resource in the ore being mined. For example, a copper ore containing 5 percent copper and 95 percent valueless rock has a grade of 5 percent. At any particular time, if all other circumstances are favorable, there is a grade below which any given mineral resource cannot be recovered economically in competition with its production from other sources. The minimum workable grade varies greatly, from about 30 percent for aluminum to as low as 0.0003 percent for platinum. It is evident in Fig. 3–5 that if we consider the ratio of the present minimum workable grade to the geochemical crustal abundance of the metal, it is the geochemically scarce metals that require the greatest concentration ratios for economic recovery. We also find that, in general, the higher the requisite concentration ratio, the fewer the number of suitable ore deposits.

Grade, although the most important factor, is not sufficient by itself to establish a workable mineral resource. The metal being recovered from an ore body, for example, must occur in a form amenable to inexpensive processing. A desired metal must not only occur in a mineral that can be inexpensively separated from its associated valueless minerals or *gangue*, to give an initial concentration or *beneficiation*, but the concentrate itself must be amenable to inexpensive, metallurgical reduction procedures to produce the metal as well. The most common classes of minerals meeting these criteria are the oxides, sulfides, native metals, and carbonates. For example, the desired minerals for the inexpensive production of iron are the oxides, magnetite (Fe_3O_4, containing 72 percent iron) or hematite (Fe_2O_3, 68 percent iron), the hydroxide goethite ($FeO \cdot OH$, 63 percent iron) or the carbonate, siderite ($FeCO_3$, 48 percent iron). But even a rich deposit of the silicate mineral almandine ($Fe_3Al_2Si_3O_{12}$) is of no interest as a source of iron, because almandine is exceedingly refractory and expensive to decompose. Indeed, it is a rare and special circumstance when a silicate, the most abundant class of minerals on the Earth, can be used as a source for any metal. On the other hand, the refractory and strength properties of silicate minerals frequently make them valuable for their nonmetallic properties. Almandine, for example, is a valuable and widely used abrasive.

Provided that the first two criteria of grade and suitable type of deposit are acceptable, a reasonably low-recovery cost must next be satisfied. This factor, of course, depends on the grade and type of the deposit, but it is also strongly dependent on the size, location, and depth of the deposit. For example, a small deposit of 10,000 tons, containing 2 ounces of gold per ton, can be profitably worked if it outcrops at the Earth's surface where costs of exploitation are low, but it cannot be profitably recovered if it lies at a depth of 2000 feet. Similarly, an oil pool of 200,000 barrels (the standard volume unit in crude oil production is the barrel, equal to 42 U.S. gallons or 158.97 liters) can be profitably sought, drilled, and pumped if it lies within a few hundred feet of the surface in a region where facilities for the collection and processing of the oil already exist. The same oil pool would not be worth recovering if it was 15,000 feet deep or was covered by 600 feet of ocean water.

An important factor in assessing the location of a deposit is its geographic position. A deposit may be so isolated and difficult of access that costs of building access ways exceed the value of the resource. It is doubtful, for example, whether even a rich metallic deposit could be profitably produced in the center of Antarctica, and the richest mines of the world could not presently make a profit if their ores were in rocks at the bottom of the deep ocean. Clearly, the costs of transporting ore to the processing and marketing sites, as well as any financing costs, taxes, and royalties that must be paid to owners of the land on which the deposit is located, must be less than the value of the material produced.

It is also important to consider the political stability and safety of the territory in which the deposit occurs,

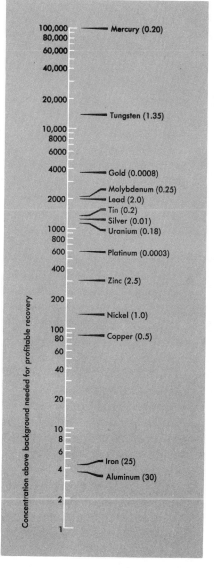

FIGURE 3-5 *To form a workable deposit, any metal must occur in a local concentration. The degree to which it must be concentrated relative to the average content of the metal in the earth's crust is shown above, together with the minimum grade that can be profitably worked by today's technology. After B. J. Skinner, 1969,* Earth Resources, *Prentice-Hall.*

FIGURE 3-6 *Before copper could be produced from the Anaconda Company's new Twin Buttes Mine in Arizona, 4½ years in planning, removal of 236 million tons of waste overburden, and construction of a mill to treat 30,000 tons of ore per day were required. This photograph shows the operation late in the preproduction stage in 1969. The mining pit is on the upper right, mill central left, and one of several overburden dumps in the foreground. The embankments enclose large areas that will be used as ponds to settle out crushed rock from the mill water after the copper minerals have been extracted. (Photograph courtesy of the Anaconda Company.)*

particularly where large-tonnage and low-grade deposits are concerned. The financial investment necessary to open a large mine, build the processing mills, erect the housing and facilities for workers in out-of-the-way regions, and construct efficient access ways may exceed $300 million (Figs. 3–6 and 3–7). This money is invested before any return is received, and many years, perhaps 15 or more, of stable, efficient operations are necessary before the investment is amortized. Political upheavals, with consequent work stoppages and unplanned interferences in the smooth-flowing operations, as well as threats of expropriation prior to amortization and returns of a reasonable profit on the investment, obviously make countries with histories of political instability unattractive sites for major investments and the production of mineral resources. The same statements are true for offshore regions controlled by politically uncertain countries and might also be true in regions of international waters unless an internationally recognized policing body can guarantee working stability.

Normally the price or value of the commodity produced, determined by the law of supply and demand, has an obvious effect on whether or not a given deposit can be economically recovered. Where a country does not contain deposits of an essential mineral commodity competitive with those in other parts of the world, however, or where suitable deposits have not yet been located, the government may still wish, for reasons of national security, to foster production within its boundaries. This end is generally accomplished by artificially raising the commodity price, either by a direct subsidy to internal producers or by acting as a central purchasing agent with contracts to internal producers at inflated prices. A good example of effective price subsidies may be seen in the development of uranium reserves during the 1950s, when the U.S. government offered long-term market contracts in a strategic move to develop its own national supplies. Prospecting for new deposits was so successful that overproduction quickly occurred.

Estimation of Resources

The estimation of a resource requires many highly subjective guesses. Where a resource can be profitably recovered by present–day technology,

FIGURE 3-7 *Some of the richest iron ores in the world lie in the arid, uninhabited Hamersley Range of Western Australia. Before the ores at Mount Whaleback and Mount Tom Price could be worked, towns had to be erected, railroads constructed over hundreds of kilometers to the coast, and major ship-loading facilities installed. The total development costs for these two mines exceeds a billion dollars.*

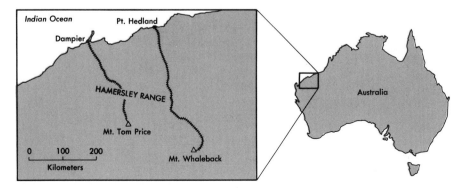

we are first of all concerned with the straightforward evaluation of how much is present. Our inability to see deep into the Earth's crust or below the ocean deeps, except by costly drilling and remote measuring procedures, means that we must resort to a good deal of geological guesswork in arriving at our conclusions. Depending on the amount of guesswork involved, we divide our estimates into three categories: If we have made all the measurements necessary to say exactly how much of the resource is present, we have a *measured reserve*. If we have only partial measurements and must make a calculated guess for the remainder, we have an *indicated reserve*. Where the estimate is based largely or entirely on geological inferences and experience, we have an *inferred reserve*.

We have qualified the use of the word reserve by saying that the resource estimated must be profitably workable by present-day technology. Many cases of identifiable concentrations of materials may eventually become profitable, however, and these cases we have already termed *potential resources*. The certainty with which we can estimate the magnitude of potential resources follows the same criteria outlined for reserves. We have, of course, an additional uncertainty. For a potential resource to become an actual resource, the necessary technological advance must occur to make recovery competitive with existing production. The farther we move from common experience, the more unconventional are the potential resources we encounter and the less reliable are our estimates of their future utility. Although we may speak favorably or unfavorably of a given potential resource from the oceans in the present context, an unanticipated technological change may eventually cause a reversal in our evaluation and change a potential resource into a reserve.

Mineral resources of the seabed

We saw in Chapter 2 that the ocean floor is divided into three major regions: the continental margin, the deep ocean floor, and the major ocean ridge systems. Each domain has different resource potentials, but it is only on the continental margin that past experience with mineral deposits helps us in making an evaluation. The reason is that, aside from surface sediments, the continental margin consists of rocks identical in all respects to those of the adjacent exposed continental mass. Therefore we can see that it is to be expected that we should observe a continuity of continental rocks and properties into the continental margins rather than encountering the submerged edge of the continent as an unusual situation. All types of mineral deposits found in continental rocks may thus be anticipated within the adjacent submerged continental margins.

Thin veneers of contemporary sediments generally form an irregular cover over the continental margins, and within these sediments, too, special classes of mineral deposits are found. By contemporary sediments we mean those deposited during the recent past, which, geologically speaking, means

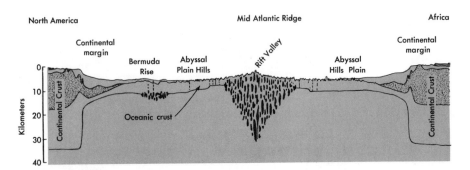

FIGURE 4-1 *Cross section of rocks underlying the Atlantic Ocean Basin, from New York to North Africa. Sediments cover the margins of the continents and the basalts composing most of the oceanic crustal rocks. The Mid-Atlantic Ridge is a site of active intrusion and extrusion of magma. After B. C. Heezer, M. Tharp, and M. Ewing, 1959, Geol. Soc. Amer., Special Paper 65.*

no more than 10 to 15 million years, during which time the present continents and ocean basins have had about the same shapes and dispositions. The contemporary sediments may be either land or shoreline materials, deposited at times of lower sea level, or they may be marine sediments formed by settling through or precipitating from sea water.

Rocks and sediments of the deep ocean floor and the major ridge system usually differ from continental materials. The processes that form them are also, at least in part, different from those forming continental rocks. The deep ocean floor and the oceanic ridges are underlain by a class of igneous rocks of volcanic origin called *basalts*, similar in composition and texture to the rocks in such volcanic islands as Hawaii, Iceland, the Azores, and Easter Island (Fig. 4–1). Basalts are dense, rather fine-grained rocks characterized by relatively high contents of such elements as magnesium, iron, and calcium and relatively low contents of silicon, aluminum, sodium, and potassium. The formative processes for basalts do not lead to the formation of many of the classes of minerals found in association with igneous rocks characteristic of the continents. The continental igneous rocks with which many ore deposits are associated are *granitic* in aspect, which means that they are not volcanic, are coarse grained, and have higher contents of silicon, aluminum, sodium, and potassium than basalts. The formative processes for granites are an integral part of mountain building, whereas those for basalts are part of the processes forming ocean basins. It is not surprising, therefore, that we expect to find different types of mineral deposits in the two regimes.

The sediments and sedimentary rocks of the deep ocean basins are also quantitatively different from sediments of the continental margins. The materials precipitating from waters in the deep ocean, whether by biological actions or chemical reactions, differ from those precipitating from the continental margins. The relative proportions of the materials from the land, transported to sea and settling through the water columns, are also different in the two cases. The types of mineral deposits to be expected in the contemporary sediments of the deep ocean floor are thus very different from those of the continental margin.

It is evident from these introductory statements that the continental margins are the oceanic sites that will most probably satisfy our demands for conventional types of mineral deposits but that the oceanic ridges and the deep ocean basins are the places where presently unconventional deposits may occur. In this chapter we attempt to assess the potential mineral resources of the three morphologically distinct oceanic provinces, with the exception of the overwhelmingly important fuel resource, petroleum, discussed separately in Chapter 5.

Resources from the Continental Margins

Metallic Mineral Deposits Within the Rocks

We might naturally expect that the most important question to ask would be whether or not mineral deposits of any sort occur in the continental margins. The question does not arise because subsea deposits discovered on land and extending under the sea have been worked for many years. Examples are the mining of iron ore beneath the seas of Finland and Canada or the recovery of tin and copper from subsea lodes off the Cornish coast of England.

The next most obvious question is whether or not the subsea deposits could be profitably worked. This factor, too, turns out not to be limiting. The technology necessary to enter the seabed by shaft or tunnel far from the shore already exists, so that standard mining operations could be carried out below depths of several hundred feet of water, entering the workings through shafts open to the atmosphere. It has been estimated by experts within the U.S. Department of the Interior that facilities to carry out such operations might be no more costly than double the equivalent installation on land.

The critical question, therefore, is not whether deposits occur or how to work them, but how do we find suitably large and rich deposits to warrant exploitation? Metallic mineral deposits occupy exceedingly small volumes compared to the volume of the geological units within which they must be sought. Location techniques must therefore be very precise. Unfortunately, most of the world's continental margins are covered by at least a few meters of contemporary sediments, and usually as much as a thousand meters, whereas metallic mineral deposits are more commonly found in the rocks below. The covering sediments and water prevent direct examinations; thus prospecting must be carried out with remote sensing devices, relying on magnetic, electrical, radioactive, or density differences between the ore deposits and their enclosing rocks. Most remote sensing is, unfortunately, unreliable for detecting metallic deposits below a few hundred feet of sediment cover. Development of deep-sensing tools for prospecting would first open unexplored parts of the dry land to more exact testing; and because any deposits discovered would generally be less expensive to explore and develop than their offshore counterparts, better prospecting methods might initially be a deterrent to offshore mining.

An increased ability to handle new types of ores and materials of lower grades is another technological development that we might suppose would hasten the day of offshore mining. In practice, the reverse may happen, with new, lower-grade resources on land proving less expensive to exploit than traditional ores under the sea because of more easily solved logistic problems on land.

We must conclude, therefore, that although the continental margins may contain rich metallic mineral deposits, they are at best potential resources and the economic drive to locate and exploit them may not occur because cheaper alternatives may be developed onshore. Should the need to develop offshore deposits arise, however, and inexpensive means for locating them be developed, existing technology is capable of allowing their exploitation.

Nonmetallic Mineral Resources Within the Rocks

The number of nonmetallic mineral resources used by man is large, but as we saw in Figure 3–3, they can be conveniently divided into four groups. Each group is at least locally important within the rocks of the continental margin, with petroleum (discussed in the next chapter) by far the most important. Building materials are most generally found in the contemporary sediments and are discussed later in this chapter, but the chemical and fertilizer compounds and water require separate discussion.

Two types of chemical and fertilizer compounds form important deposits within the continental margins: phosphorite deposits, which are the principal source of our phosphatic fertilizers, and the compounds found in marine evaporite deposits and the so-called salt domes that arise from them. Extensive experience on the geological properties of both types of deposit has been gained by working similar deposits on the coastal plains where they provide the sites for the extraction, or potential extraction, of common salt, potassium salts (potentially), sulfur from salt domes, and phosphate.

The salt domes that are so important for the exploitation of salt and sulfur are the expression of a peculiar condition of sedimentary history and the subsequent physical constraints on a pile of ancient sediments. In order to evaluate these important resources, we must look a little closer at the geologic circumstances covering them.

Through geological time, shallow marine embayments and basins with restricted water flows but high rates of surface evaporation have been formed by the onlap of oceans onto the continental masses. At times this action appears to have been connected with the beginnings of a new rift related to the large-scale plate tectonics mentioned earlier. Continued inflow and evaporation eventually produce thick beds of sea salts from tens to thousands of meters thick (Fig. 4–2). The order in which compounds precipitate from the evaporating sea water are, first, calcium carbonate ($CaCO_3$), then calcium sulfate ($CaSO_4$) or the hydrated counterpart $CaSO_4 \cdot 2H_2O$ (depending on temperature) and sodium chloride (NaCl), and, finally, a complex mixture of potassium and magnesium compounds, including salts like KCl, and $KCl_3Mg \cdot 6H_2O$. This evaporation sequence is also used in obtaining solar salts, as discussed in Chapter 6. The evaporation cycle may be broken anywhere in the chain by the introduction of additional sea water, and most marine evaporite basins do not reach the stage where the potassium salts appear.

The evaporite beds, as the layers of precipitated salts are called, may reach a thousand meters or more in thickness but are more often only a few tens or hundred meters thick. The basin within which evaporites are deposited is commonly formed during tectonic plate movements as the first down-buckling, or thinning, of a section of continental crust. After deposition of the evaporites, the basin may continue to deepen, and the evaporites become covered by an even thicker layer of detrital sediments, such as sandstones and mudstones. Were it not for salt domes, much of the evaporite deposit would lie at impossibly great depths for mining.

Common salt (NaCl), the major constituent of most marine evaporites, has a density of 2.2 grams/cc, whereas the associated clay and sand-rich sedimentary rocks overlying and underlying them have densities of at least 2.5 grams. Salt is capable of plastic flow, like the ice in a glacier, and, being lighter than the overlying rocks, tends to rise and flow upward in long, thin columns or plugs, puncturing and piercing the mechanically weak sedi-

FIGURE 4-2 *Cross section of a basin with restricted flow leading to the accumulation of salt deposits. Fresh sea water flows over a bar and is concentrated by evaporation. The dense brine formed by evaporation sinks and is prevented from returning to the open sea by the bar. When the brine reaches a high enough salinity, salts start to precipitate and may eventually fill the basin.*

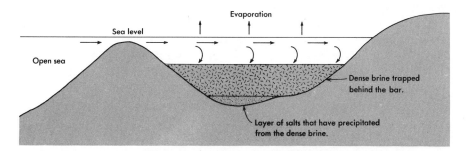

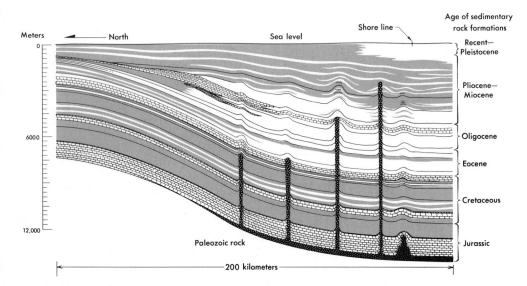

FIGURE 4-3 *Salt domes, narrow pluglike columns of salt that rise and "flow" upward through heavier but mechanically weak overlying rocks, doming and eventually rupturing them as they rise. By this mechanism, deeply buried salt from marine evaporite deposits can reach the surface. This geologic section of eastern Louisiana shows known salt domes that are believed to have risen through as much as 40,000 feet of overlying sediments. After J. Ben Carsey, 1950, Bull. Amer. Assoc. Petroleum Geologists, v. 34, p. 362.*

ments and doming the strata above (Fig. 4–3). It is in recognition of the domed rocks over the salt plugs, that the columns are called *salt domes*. They are known to have risen through as much as 12 kilometers of overlying sediments and range in diameter from a few hundred meters to more than two kilometers.

The presence of salt domes on several continental margins has now been demonstrated by geophysical methods. Off the northwest coast of Africa, for example, a large number of pluglike bodies have been discovered piercing the overlying sediments, and they are particularly abundant within the Gulf of Mexico (Fig. 4–4). These domes, and any others discovered on the continental shelves or slopes, can be considered at least potential resources of salt. The potential is an exceedingly long-term one, however, because salt beds with readily recovered reserves measured in trillions of tons have been found on most continents.

Although salt from salt domes still seems a distant possibility, another nonmetallic resource associated with salt domes is a very real and current possibility—sulfur. A rising salt dome carries with it any other materials present in the deeply buried evaporite horizons. One relatively abundant compound is anhydrite ($CaSO_4$). As the salt dome nears the surface, it reaches a zone where deep-circulating ground waters will dissolve the uppermost layers of salt, leaving a growing residue, or *cap rock*, of the relatively insoluble anhydrite (Fig. 4–5). The upturned strata around the salt

FIGURE 4-4 *Known and probable salt domes (white dots and open circles, respectively) identified in the coastal area of the Gulf of Mexico. In no other part of the world has such a profusion of these unusual bodies been identified. (Adaption from Grover E. Murray, 1961,* Geology of the Atlantic and Gulf Coastal Province of North America, *Harper and Row.*

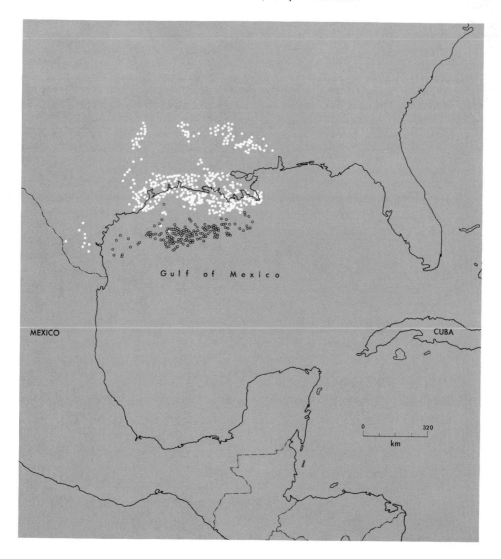

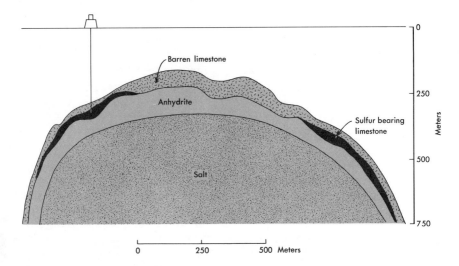

FIGURE 4-5 *The capping of relatively insoluble anhydrite (CaSO₄) that has ac-cumulated at the top of the Hoskins Mound Salt Dome, Texas, when deep, cir-culating water dissolved out some of the salt. The limestone and sulfur were de-rived from the anhydrite by the action of bacteria as explained in the text. The drilling platform is drawn to scale and is about the same size as those shown in Figure 4-7. After A. H. Marx, 1936, "Hoskins Mound Salt Dome, Brazoria County, Texas," in* Gulf Coast Oil Fields, *Amer. Assoc. Petroleum Geologists.*

intrusion also act as sites for the accumulation of petroleum hydrocarbons. About a thousand meters below the surface, a special class of anaerobic bacteria, capable of reducing sulfate to sulfide and of metabolizing the oil, may percolate into the cap rock. Reactions of the following type occur:

$$CaSO_4 + CH_4 \xrightarrow{\substack{\text{bacteria} \\ \text{in the} \\ \text{presence} \\ \text{of water}}} CaCO_3 + H_2S + H_2O$$

anhydrite   hydro-   calcite   gas   water
            carbon

As the hydrogen sulfide bubbles upward and reaches layers containing dissolved oxygen in the downward-percolating ground water, it is oxidized to elemental sulfur:

$$2H_2S + O_2 \longrightarrow 2H_2O + 2S.$$

Both the calcium carbonate and the sulfur formed by these reactions will be distributed through the cap rock. If the sulfur concentration becomes high enough, it can be recovered by a special drilling process known as the Frasch process (Fig. 4–6). Superheated water and air are forced down a drill hole, melting the sulfur and forming a froth of air bubbles, molten sulfur, and water that is light enough to return by gravity up another hole or the outer portion of the same hole.

Two large salt domes off the Louisiana coast are now producing sulfur. One, the Grand Isle dome, has been producing for many years (Fig. 4-7), whereas a second, the Cominda Pass dome, started producing in 1968. Their combined reserves are inferred to be close to 35 million tons. In total, nearly 200 million tons of sulfur have already been produced from salt domes in the coastal region of the Gulf of Mexico, and the ultimate production will certainly be much larger.

The frequency with which exploitable sulfur is found in the cap rock of salt domes is low. Although nearly 350 salt domes have been found to date in the Gulf coastal region, both on- and offshore, only 7 percent is known to contain—or have contained—economically recoverable quantities

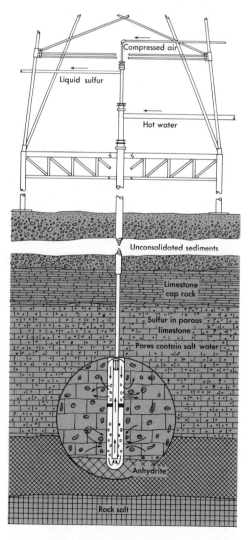

FIGURE 4-6 *The Frasch method of recovering sulfur. Superheated water and compressed air are forced down a drill hole, causing the sulfur to melt and form a froth of air bubbles, molten sulfur, and water, which is light enough to return by gravity up a central pipe. After the Texas Gulf Sulphur Co.*

Compressed air

Liquid sulfur

Hot water

Unconsolidated sediments

Limestone cap rock

Sulfur in porous limestone

Pores contain salt water

Anhydrite

Rock salt

FIGURE 4-7 *Sulfur being produced by the Frasch process from the Grand Isle dome off the Louisiana coast. This installation was opened by the Freeport Sulphur Company in 1960. The power plant to produce hot water is at the left and the producing platforms are at the ends of the three arms. The platform at upper right is the site of a drill hole that drains any excess mining water from the sulfur deposit. (Photograph courtesy of the Freeport Sulphur Company.)*

of sulfur, with an additional 2 percent containing uneconomic amounts. Unfortunately, the frequency of sulfur-bearing salt domes seems to be less offshore than onshore. The reasons for this distribution are uncertain but appear to be related to the presence of suitable fresh ground waters to form the initial cap rock and possibly also to promote oxidation of the H_2S. The existence of sulfur-bearing domes on other continental shelves remains to be determined.

No large reserves of potassium salts have ever been found in salt domes, either on- or offshore, but geologists in the U.S. Geological Survey have reported finding the mineral sylvite (KCl) in some of the salt domes rising through the coastal plain fringing the Gulf of Mexico. These domes rise from the Louanne salt beds deposited over 150 million years ago in the Jurassic age, approximately 40,000 feet below the surface of the Gulf. Many scientists consider it a good possibility that eventually a potash-rich salt dome might be discovered among the hundreds now known in the region.

The other deposits of economic interest in the continental margin are the phosphorus-rich deposits called *phosphorites.* The calcium phosphate mineral apatite, having the ideal formula $Ca_5(PO_4)_3F_2$, is the common phosphorus compound in the Earth's crust. Apatite itself is not a readily soluble mineral—indeed its low solubility contributes to its accumulation as a precipitate on the sea floor—but it is readily converted to soluble compounds by treatment with sulfuric acid, to form the well-known fertilizer, *superphosphate*.

Apatite is widely spread as crusts, pellets, nodules, and even skeletal remains of vertebrate animals across the ocean floor, but particularly on certain continental shelves. The apatitic nodules and crusts, commonly called phosphorite, contain additional elements in the crystal lattice besides those of the ideal formula. Phosphorite therefore has a variable composition and is generally expressed by the formula $Ca_5(PO_4,CO_3)_3$ $(F,Cl,OH)_2$. It is standard analytical practice to report phosphate contents of ores as the oxide P_2O_5 rather than as PO_4, and the apatites in phosphorites range in their P_2O_5 contents from 36 to 40 percent by weight. Unfortunately, the crusts, nodules, and pellets found on the ocean floor contain an abundant admixture of other minerals that lower the P_2O_5 contents below 30 percent and, in many cases, below 20 percent. Because these admixed minerals cannot be inexpensively removed, the marine phosphorites have not yet become economically competitive with terrestrial supplies in which P_2O_5 contents exceed 30 percent, or for which inexpensive concentration schemes are available.

The tonnages of phosphorite on or close to the sea floor, and therefore accessible by dredging operations, are enormous (Fig. 4–8). The largest known tonnages are on the East and West coasts of North America, but exploration of other continental margins will probably reveal large deposits in other parts of the world. It is estimated that, off the coast of Southern California and that portion of Mexico known as Baja California, 25,000 km²

FIGURE 4-8   *Offshore areas in which deposits of phosporite are known to occur. After U.S. Geological Survey, 1970.*

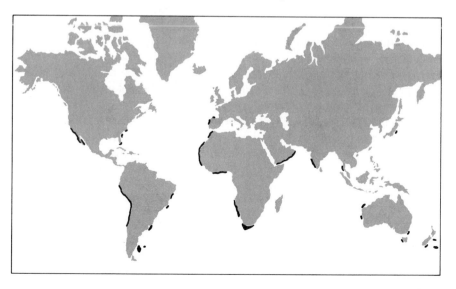

of the sea floor contain phosphorite nodules lying on the bottom, most of which is no deeper than 550 meters. From these figures, it was estimated in 1965 that at least 100 million tons of phosphate might be recovered.

Phosphorites are also known to occur in scattered deposits from Cape Cod to Miami along the broad continental margin of eastern North America. The same region is characterized by phosphorite deposits outcropping on land; and, in parallel with the land deposits, the richest submarine phosphorites are to be found between Virginia and Florida. The water depths range from 60 to 2200 meters, and the total area over which phosphorite is known exceeds 125,000 km². Clearly, the deposits are again enormous, and although grades are below 20 percent P_2O_5, the potential resources can be inferred to be in the billions of tons.

Although the phosphorite deposits are widespread along the North American continental margins, they are not modern deposits that are forming today. Rather, they are surficial deposits formed by weathering and erosion of phosphatic-rich beds formed during the Miocene Epoch, between 7 and 26 million years ago. The same Miocene phosphatic beds outcrop on land, and in Florida and Tennessee large deposits of rich phosphorite are worked. Indeed, the Florida phosphate deposits are the largest producers of phosphatic fertilizers in the world.

With such large tonnages of phosphorite close to shore, much of it within reach by dredging techniques now technically feasible, it is pertinent to ask why marine phosphorites have not yet been exploited. The answer lies first in their grade. They are not quite as rich as their equivalents on shore, where various weathering processes have served to enrich the initial marine sedimentary phosphorites. The second part of the answer lies in the tonnages available on land. With a world production of almost 100 million tons per year, the United States alone has rich on-land phosphate deposits with indicated reserves of 14,500 million tons, and those of Morocco, where the world's largest known reserves reside, are at least 50 percent larger.

The final important nonmetallic mineral from the continental margins is fresh water, a substance that many of us scarcely think of as a mineral. Fresh water is less dense than salty sea water and tends to float on the surface, as is so commonly observed in estuaries. In the open sea, wave action eventually mixes the two water bodies. If fresh water is confined to an underground aquifer, however, mixing does not occur so readily. Where porous rock strata outcrop on land but dip out beneath the sea below impermeable strata, fresh water may be forced down the porous aquifer and may form a wedge of fresh water floating on the salty water that saturates the strata at depth. The greater the head of water on land (meaning the higher the point of intake above sea level), the greater will be the depth of the freshwater wedge beneath the sea. This principle is the same one we observe in icebergs.

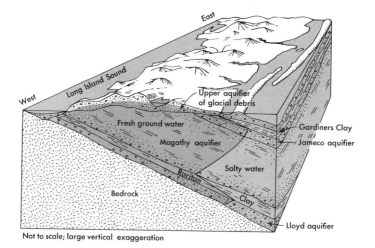

West

East

Long Island Sound

Upper aquifer of glacial debris

Fresh ground water

Gardiners Clay

Magothy aquifer

Jameco aquifer

Raritan

Salty water

Bedrock

Clay

Lloyd aquifer

Not to scale; large vertical exaggeration

FIGURE 4-9   *Ground water occurs in several porous aquifers below Long Island. The uppermost aquifer is a veneer of glacial debris. Below it the sand and gravel beds known as the Jameco, Magothy, and Lloyd aquifers dip out to sea at a shallow angle. Rain water falling on Long Island enters the aquifers and floats as a wedge of fresh water on the salty sea water that saturates the beds at depth. Water in these aquifers provides a principle water supply for Long Island's large population. After* New York Water Resources Bulletin 62A, 1970.

For many coastal communities, the availability of water from aquifers that dip out under the continental shelf is vitally important. The large New York population on Long Island, for example, relies heavily on water from layers of sand and gravel, called the Lloyd, Magothy, and Jameco aquifers, that dip southward under the sea (Fig. 4–9). The continental margin thus serves as a water reservoir for Long Island and many other coastal communities. The same principle operates on oceanic islands, even though no continental margin is present. On the island of Oahu, Hawaii, for example, the extensive population relies heavily on a water lens confined within the porous volcanic rocks that make up the island.

The rate at which water is withdrawn from a subsea reservoir is obviously a critical question. If the withdrawal rate exceeds the input rate, the salty water will rise within the aquifer, and eventually coastal wells will be pumping undesirable salt water. Wise and cooperative communal management of rich water supplies is therefore vital.

Metallic Mineral Deposits in the Contemporary Sedimentary Cover

Most minerals are not stable at the Earth's surface, being slowly decomposed by weathering to finer-grained products such as clays. Some materials, however, are very resistant to chemical weathering. If they are further resistant to mechanical abrasion and have a relatively higher density than quartz and clay, then water and wind actions cause separations between

Mineral resources of the seabed

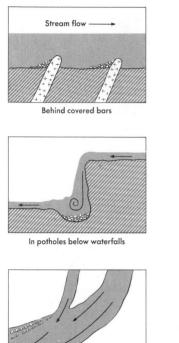

Behind covered bars

In covered rock holes

In potholes below waterfalls

On the inside of meander loops

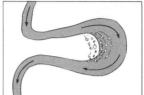

Stream flow →

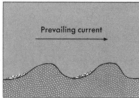

Prevailing current →

Downstream from the
mouth of a tributary

In the ocean behind bars against
the prevailing current

FIGURE 4-10 *Typical sites for placer accumulations, which occur where obstructing or deflecting barriers allow faster-moving waters to carry away the suspended load of light and fine-grained material while trapping the more dense and coarse particles that are moving along the bottom by rolling or partial suspension. Placers may form wherever water occurs, although they are most commonly associated with streams and nearshore marine currents.*

Table 4–1

The Heavy Minerals Commonly Recovered from Detrital Deposits

Mineral	Composition	Density, grams/cc	Principal Form Used	Type of Detrital Deposit
Gold	Au	19.3	Metallic gold	Stream and offshore
Platinum	Pt with Pd, Os, Rh, Ir, etc.	14–19	Metallic platinum	Stream
Cassiterite	SnO_2	7.0	Metallic tin	Stream and offshore
Wolframite	$FeWO_4$	7.5	Metallic tungsten	Stream
Columbite-tantalite	$Fe(Nb, Ta)_2O_8$	5–8	Metallic niobium and tantalum	Stream
Magnetite	Fe_3O_4	5.2	Metallic iron	Offshore
Chromite	$FeCr_2O_4$	4.5	Metallic chromium	Stream and offshore
Rutile	TiO_2	4.3	Titanium oxide	Offshore
Ilmenite	$FeTiO_3$	4.7	Titanium oxide	Offshore
Monazite	Rare-earth phosphate	5.0	Rare-earth chemicals	Offshore
Zircon	$ZrSiO_4$	4.7	Zirconium silicate	Offshore
Ruby and sapphire	Al_2O_3	4.0	Gems	Stream
Diamond	C	3.5	Gems	Stream and offshore

Mineral resources of the seabed

the "heavy" residues and the lighter alteration products. The concentrations of heavy residues are called *detrital* deposits. Where extensive winnowing by stream waters or near-shore currents occurs (Fig. 4–10), detrital deposits of tough, heavy, and resistant minerals may become very rich. Table 4–1 lists the heavy minerals now being exploited from detrital deposits. Many

FIGURE 4-11   *Offshore dredging operations for the recovery of cassiterite (SnO$_2$) near Thailand. The top photograph shows the first such dredge in Thailand in 1907, when cassiterite could be recovered in relatively shallow water. A bucket line dredged gravels up from the left. They were then processed and dumped back to the sea via the boom on the right. The bottom photograph shows a modern dredge owned by the Tongkah Harbour Tin Dredging Co., capable of working in much deeper and more open sea water. The dredge line is entering the sea on the right and the disposal boom is on the left. (Photographs courtesy of Dept. of Mineral Resources, Bangkok, Thailand.)*

such deposits are found in the sediments of continental margins, and within these deposits are located the potential metallic mineral resources most likely to be exploited in the oceans in the foreseeable future. Indeed, some offshore detrital deposits, such as tin off Thailand and Indonesia (Fig. 4–11), and rutile and zircon off Australia, are currently being mined, and thus fall in the category of measured reserves.

We may conveniently subdivide detrital deposits into two classes: first, those where stream waters have served as the concentrating medium and, second, those where currents in the ocean have effected the concentration. Deposits in the first category are far more abundant than those in the second.

Many detrital deposits now located on the continental shelf are simply stream-derived deposits formed when the ocean level was lower during

FIGURE 4-12   *Placer tin deposits were formed when cassiterite (SnO₂) was concentrated in the streams draining the island of Singkep in Indonesia. The concentration occurred during a period of low sea level in the Pleistocene Era. With the rise of sea level to its present stand, many of the placers have been submerged and must be worked by offshore dredging. The distribution of cassiterite still reflects its old stream channels. After P. H. Zaalberg, 1970, "Offshore tin dredging in Indonesia,"* Transactions of the Institution of Mining and Metallurgy, Section A, v. 79, p. A86.

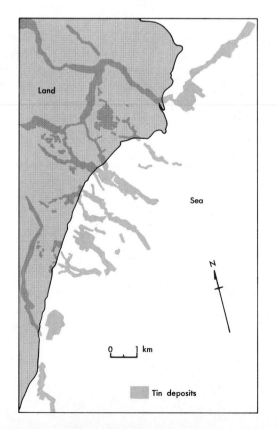

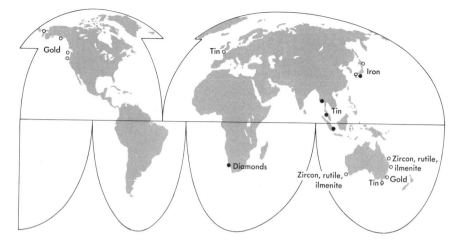

FIGURE 4-13 *Areas of the world where offshore mining of heavy minerals from placer deposits is currently active or where recent pro prospecting gives promise of production in the near future. After K. O. Emery and L. C. Noakes, 1968, "Economic placer deposits of the continental shelf" in Technical Bulletin, ECAFE, v. 1, p. 95.*

times of worldwide glaciation. A classic example is to be found in the detrital tin deposits of the Far East, a major source of the world's tin deposits. Cassiterite (SnO_2), formed when granites were intruded during the Cretaceous Period, from 65 to 136 million years ago, occurs in veins that have been subsequently elevated and subjected to deep tropical weathering. Being resistant to erosion, cassiterite is concentrated locally on the surface when clays and other alteration minerals are washed away. The residual concentration process was particularly effective along valley walls, but any cassiterite grains reaching the valley floor were further concentrated in detrital stream deposits. The drainage channels we now see are only the headwaters of what were much more extensive Pleistocene and earlier river systems formed at times of lower sea level, and it is along these now drowned drainage channels that offshore tin is dredged from water depths as great as 40 meters (Fig. 4-12).

Detrital deposits formed directly by movement of ocean waters are confined to the near-shore or beach zone, where longshore currents and the washing of water across the beach zone are sufficiently vigorous to separate light minerals, such as quartz and feldspar (density ranging from 2.6 to 2.8), from heavy minerals, such as ilmenite, rutile, zircon, and monazite. Frequent reworking of old beach deposits by wave action as the sea level rises has produced a number of rich detrital deposits. Although rarely as rich as their stream-derived counterparts, the beach deposits may be very extensive. Indeed, the world's major source of zircon and rutile is from beach sands along the eastern coast of Australia (Fig. 4–13). The opportunity for repeated reworking is an important aspect in the formation of beach deposits and accounts for the common observation that modern beach deposits are generally richer than deposits in drowned and submerged beaches where dissection and further reworking have occurred. During periods of sea-level lowering, however, rich beach deposits may be left stranded in fossil shorelines.

Interesting and unique detrital deposits of diamonds occur in South West Africa, between Luderitz Bay and the Orange River. Ancient rivers in the area carried diamond-bearing gravels from primary sources in the interior of southern Africa to the sea. Current and wave action then deposited the gravels along the coast as a series of beach terraces. Most of the beach terraces are now exposed, but some are submerged, thus making it necessary to employ floating dredges to recover the gravels from the ocean floor. These deposits are also unusual for another reason. Although primary diamond deposits have a high percentage of industrial diamonds that are unsuitable for use as gems, the detrital beach deposits yield approximately 97 percent gem quality diamonds. This extremely high percentage is believed due to the pounding received by the diamonds from gravels and boulders during their long river transport and subsequent beach deposition. Tests have shown that nearly perfect gem crystals resist the pounding much better than the imperfectly crystalline industrial diamonds.

The current beach and offshore production of detrital minerals around the world amounts to approximately 7 percent of all detrital mineral production, for an annual value of about $50 million. Potential resources, especially of ilmenite, rutile, and magnetite are large, however. Approximately 50 percent of the inferred reserves of ilmenite in the United States, for example, occurs in fossil beach deposits in Florida, and the possibilities of finding additional large deposits offshore are high. Because of the need for strong wave and current action to effect concentrations, it is unlikely that detrital deposits will be discovered beyond 200 meters water depth; but even with this limitation, potential resources of ilmenite along the Atlantic coastal shelf of the United States may be as large as 10^9 tons, more than ten times as large as the onshore resources. The potentials of most continental margins have not been tested, or, at best, they have been tested in a rudimentary fashion. We suspect that production of detrital deposits along the continental margins will grow rapidly during the decades ahead as exploration of the shelves proceeds.

Nonmetallic Mineral Resources in the Contemporary Sediment Cover

Only two general classes of nonmetallic mineral resources are recovered from the contemporary cover of the continental margins—building materials and agricultural soil conditioners. The soil conditioner used is calcium carbonate, found in shells, lime muds, corals, and other marine deposits. Because some calcium carbonate-bearing materials are also widely used for building materials, it is convenient to combine them rather than discuss them separately. It is also convenient to subdivide the building materials into two subgroups. The first includes those that are used directly as they come from the ground, without any treatment or change beyond shaping, such as is involved in crushing, sieving, and cutting. The second group includes materials that must be treated chemically, fired, melted, mixed with other materials, or otherwise altered so that they can be molded and set into new forms. The first group includes sand, gravel, crushed stone, and cut stone, whereas the second includes cement, plaster, asbestos, glass, and ceramic clays.

Several important features characterize the building materials, but two are of paramount importance. They all have high per capita consumption rates (the per capita consumption rate of sand and gravel in the United States is approximately 4 tons per year), which means that deposits must be large if they are to be of economic interest. Second, they all have low unit costs, which means that their value in the ground is low, on the order of $1 per ton. If materials are to be priced at a few dollars a ton at the building site, neither transportation nor production costs can be very high. These factors tend to defeat submarine production of most building material resources, and, with two exceptions, offshore production of building materials holds little or no interest.

The most important exception is sand and gravel. With increasing population densities in the high-latitude coastal areas above about 40 degrees, onshore sources of sand and gravel are being rapidly depleted. It is precisely in these high latitudes, however, that extensive sand and gravel deposits occur on the continental margins. In North America and Europe, particularly England and Denmark, an estimated $100 million worth was already being recovered annually by 1970.

The origins of the high-latitude sand and gravel deposit lie in the recently passed glacial period. At the time of maximum glaciation, the ice sheets extended to the edge of the continental margin. As the ice retreated, it left extensive piles of rock fragments, both by direct dumping to form moraines and by transportation and deposition by glacial streams fed from melt waters. These deposits now blanket the continental shelf and slope, submerged by the rising sea level. Similar glacial debris is, of course, scattered across the old glaciated land surface, but most of the accessible materials adjacent to populous areas, such as the northeastern United States, have already been recovered.

Sand-sized particles are more easily dispersed than gravel boulders. Although there are almost continuous sand deposits from Maine to Florida along the Atlantic coastal shelf, gravels are much more restricted (Fig. 4–14). Deposits of sand are almost incalculably large, and because they can be recovered by simple dredging operations, we may confidently pre-

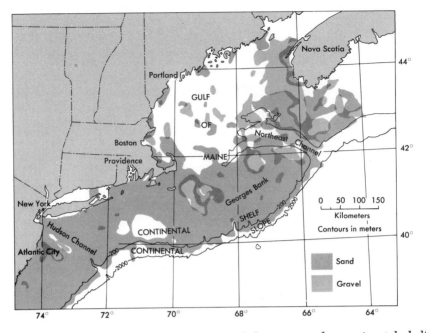

FIGURE 4-14 *Distribution of sand and gravel deposits on the continental shelf off northeastern United States. Gravel means that more than 25 percent of the particles in the deposit have a diameter greater than 1 mm, sand means that 50 percent or more of the particles have diameters between 1/16 and 1 mm. When more than 50 percent of the particles are below 1/16 mm in diameter, the deposit is classed as mud. After U.S. Geol. Surv., Circular 602.*

dict an increasing exploitation off the northeastern United States. Deposits of gravel in the region are not as large, but they can be inferred to be in the tens of billions of tons and thus of tremendous potential importance for coastal communities.

Gravel deposits are sparse or absent off many tropical and subtropical coasts. Along the northern margin of the Gulf of Mexico, for example, although sands are found, particularly in the fans of river deltas, gravels are almost unknown. The only coarse building aggregates under the circumstances are old shell beds, particularly oyster shells, clam shells, and coral reefs.

Shells and corals lack the high strength of gravels and crushed rock but are considerably lighter because they are porous. Consequently, concrete prepared from them has desirable weight properties but is less strong. Oyster shells are widely used around the world. In Texas and Louisiana, for example, these shells continue to be the major concrete aggregate and road-building base used. Most of the onshore supplies have already been depleted, and all further production will occur offshore. Clam shells, although not so widely used, are also important and in some areas, such as southern Alabama, are the major building material.

The same marine shells and corals, as well as lime muds and recent limestones, also provide calcium carbonate ($CaCO_3$) to be used as a source of agricultural lime for controlling soil acidity and for furnishing a vital source of calcium for plant growth. These marine sources are also effective supplies of lime for cement manufacture where alternate sources are not available.

Reserves of recoverable calcium carbonate on the continental margins of the world are enormous, for it is on the margins that much of the limestone forms. The deterrent to offshore production, however, is onshore abundance. Limestones and marbles are so widely scattered on the continents that it is generally easier and cheaper to open an onshore quarry close to the demand than it is to dredge the material offshore. For agricultural purposes, transportation costs are again the limiting factor.

Two special circumstances provide obvious exceptions to the preceding statements. On volcanic islands, such as Hawaii, and along coasts where igneous rocks predominate, limestones are rare; therefore shoreline or off-shore shell beds and coral reefs are the only local sources of agricultural lime, as well as lime for cement manufacture. Another exception is found in the sea around the Bahama Islands, where a fine-grained and pure form of calcium carbonate is deposited. This material can be worked inexpensively, shipped by cheap water transport to coastal areas of eastern North America, and under some circumstances, sold competitively with local onshore supplies.

Resources From the Spreading Edges of Plates

When we attempt to assess the potential resources of the oceanic ridge system, we are dealing with a province that is still little known to science and industry. The oceanic ridge is the greatest mountain chain on Earth, but only rarely, in isolated volcanic islands, does it penetrate the ocean surface. Thus most of our direct information has come from dredging, drilling, and geophysical observations; consequently, our estimates of its resource potentials are mostly geological guesswork. The few clues we have, however, do not lead us to predict a cornucopia of riches.

Deposits Associated with Igneous Rocks

Most classes of metallic mineral deposits exploited on land are associated with igneous, metamorphic, or sedimentary rocks that are not known to form along the oceanic ridge system. Certain kinds of deposits, however, could theoretically form in the oceanic ridge, for the ridge is being built from igneous material that is largely basaltic in composition and that is supplied from the Earth's mantle. Large volumes of molten basalt (more correctly called basaltic magma), when allowed to cool slowly after injection into the crust, will naturally be differentiated as the result of gravitational sinking of the early formed crystals to the floor of the magma chamber or cavity into which the injection occurred. The reason is that most crystals are more dense than their parent liquid. By gravitational differentiation, an initially homogeneous magma may cool to form a series of distinctive layers, each characterized by its own set of minerals. By differentiation, metals that only occur in trace amounts in the parent magma may be concentrated in specific layers that are sufficiently enriched to warrant their exploitation by mining.

Copper and nickel deposits in the Sudbury, Ontario, district of Canada, and copper, nickel, platinum, and chromium deposits in the Bushveldt Igneous complex of South Africa are believed to have formed in just this fashion. The igneous rock types of the ocean basins and oceanic ridges are appropriate for crystal settling, but incessant earth motion or tectonic activity, associated with the continual injection of new magma along the oceanic ridges, reduces the probability of slow, undisturbed cooling and gravitative settling necessary to effect the concentration. A further drawback in searching for deposits of this type is that they apparently form within the crust rather than on it. Erosional forces acting on the oceanic ridges are weaker than the strong tectonic movements and the deposits are therefore unlikely to be exposed and discovered. The only possibility appears to lie in transform fault movements dissecting the ocean floor, where the large-scale horizontal and vertical movements that occur may expose a deposit by chance. Rock types displaying gravitational settling features have been dredged from the deep fracture zone known as the Romanche Trench.

One other type of metallic mineral deposit remains as a possibility in the oceanic ridge system. Metamorphism, or alteration, of basaltic igneous rocks, particularly in the presence of saline waters to serve as a solvent and transporting agent, may sometimes lead to the formation of copper deposits. Examples of deposits of this type, formed in a fragment of metamorphosed ocean crust now tectonically elevated above sea level, are to be found in Newfoundland, and in Cyprus where copper has been mined from prehistoric times. Indeed, the word "cyprus" means *copper* in Greek. The possibility must be entertained that similar deposits could have formed or could be forming along the oceanic ridges, where faulting and other tectonic breaks might allow deep infiltration of sea water and where the intense volcanic activity provides a source of heat to effect the metamorphism.

There are, therefore, two possible classes of metallic ore deposits that may occur in the igneous rocks of the oceanic ridges. Because of ocean-floor spreading, the entire basaltic crust was at one time at a site of intense volcanic activity along a ridge, so that, in principle, both types of ore deposits might also be distributed throughout the deep ocean floor. The possibilities of finding them, however, are remote. Where the ocean ridges and portions of the ocean basin floor project above sea level, as in Iceland and Hawaii, no suggestions of metallic mineral deposits are to be found. The search must therefore be made underwater for deposits, and here we face the problem of the mantle of sedimentary rocks. Most of the ocean floor is mantled by a cover of loosely consolidated sediments averaging a few hundred meters thick. Remote sensing devices are unlikely ever to be precise enough to penetrate such a cover of water and sediment, and even if we limited our search to the flanks of the ridge, where the sediment veneer is thin, combinations of adverse factors make the probability of discovery and exploitation exceedingly low.

Deposits Associated with New Rifts and Rifts Adjacent to Continents

The tectonic plates presently moving on the Earth are not the only plates to have formed during geological history. Plates apparently form and are consumed continually. Where a new plate is forming, a spreading center may open under a continent. Before the continent is actually split apart with the initiation of processes typical of the oceanic crust described above, a period of time elapses during which the continental crust is thinned and warped. In some cases, there is evidence that shallow seas that are the sites of evaporite deposits and other shallow water deposits are formed as discussed previously. The crustal thinning may then be followed by numerous bodies of magma rising from the mantle and being intruded at the site of spreading. The igneous intrusions heat any waters present, and hot ground waters percolating through the thinning cover of continental rocks leach the trace amounts of heavy metals present. It is possible that they may also collect any heavy metals released by the magma, thereby serving as effective ore-forming solutions from two possible sources. Because the initial ground water is probably sea water, and because the evaporites in the section may increase their salinity, conditions for transporting heavy metals, such as copper, lead, and zinc, are optimal.

FIGURE 4-15 *A generalized section across the Red Sea showing igneous rocks at the spreading center bounded by block of continental crust dropped down as a veneer of sediments. After C. L. Drake, 1972, "Future considerations concerning geodynamics," Bull. Amer. Assoc. Petroleum Geologists, v. 56, p. 260.*

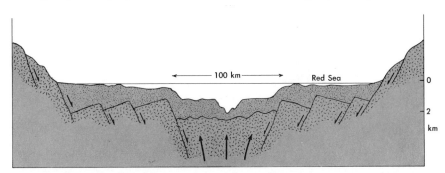

Such a situation seems to be the case in the Red Sea, which is the site of active splitting apart of continental crust (Fig. 4–15). An extension of the oceanic ridge of the Indian Ocean is splitting Arabia away from Africa. The Red Sea is still underlain by continental crustal rocks, including salt beds, and the igneous activity along the ridge axis has apparently caused deep-seated waters, probably either sea water or fresh waters entering aquifers on land, to circulate and to become more saline by solution of bedded salt deposits. The hot brines react with rocks they are passing through, causing elements like copper, lead, and zinc to become concentrated in the brine. The hot brines eventually make their way to the sea floor, and, being more dense than sea water, have formed unusual stratified pools. Four such pools have now been located in the Red Sea (Fig. 4–16). The brines themselves are not generally considered as a resource despite their high metal concentrations, but the metal-rich sediments underlying the brine pools are potential resources. By some process not yet fully understood, the metal-charged brines precipitate much of their dissolved metal load as the sulfides of copper, zinc, and iron into the fine-grained, loosely

FIGURE 4-16 *Location of the four deep, hot, metal-rich brine pools in the Red Sea. Three deeps, the Atlantis II, Chain, and Discovery deeps, are very close together. After Ross, Hays, and Allstrom, in* Hot Brines and Recent Heavy Metal Deposits in the Red Sea, a Geochemical and Geophysical Account, *E. T. Degens and D. A. Ross, 1969, Springer-Verlag.*

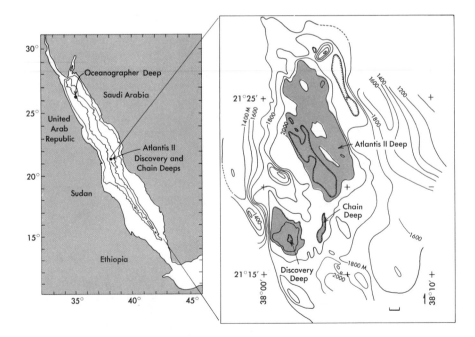

Mineral resources of the seabed

Table 4–2

A Typical Analysis of a Mud from the Atlantis II Deep in the Red Sea*

Metal	Weight Percent
Manganese	0.12
Lead	0.16
Copper	0.70
Zinc	2.06

*After J. C. Bischoff, "Red Sea geothermal brine deposits: Their mineralogy, chemistry, and genesis," in E. T. Degens and D. A. Ross, 1969, *Hot Brines and Recent Heavy Metal Deposits in the Red Sea*, published by Springer-Verlag, New York.

consolidated sediments on the sea floor, forming extensive and rich deposits. It has been estimated, for example, that the Atlantis II deep is underlain by 53 km² of sediments to a depth of 10 meters and that all of the sediments may contain potentially exploitable concentrations of copper and zinc. A typical analysis of Red Sea brine pool muds is given in Table 4–2.

Both the large tonnage present and the metal concentration of the muds indicate potentially rich resources. Nevertheless, there are several drawbacks to their exploitation. First, the muds and the sulfide minerals they contain are so fine grained that present metallurgical practice could not treat them successfully. Even similar deposits on shore would probably be too fine grained for exploitation. The same problem, as we shall see, burdens the exploitable potential of manganese nodules on the deep ocean floor. Second, the deposits lie below several hundred meters of sea water, and entirely new mining methods must be devised before recovery could proceed. Finally, and perhaps in the long run most importantly, it is not clear to whom the deposits belong, and until agreement is reached on ownership of oceanic resources, no one is likely to attempt expensive recovery lest they lose their entire endeavor.

If the formative process outlined above is established as uniquely determining for this kind of deposit, then similar deposits are only likely in areas of spreading plates that are still covered by or close to the continental blocks being pushed apart. In addition to the Red Sea, the only other site suggesting itself as a current possibility is the Gulf of California. Indeed, an apparently similar metal-rich brine was hit by a deep well in 1963 near the Salton Sea in the Imperial Valley of Southern California, which is an onshore continuation of the rift forming the Gulf of California. Conceivably, other brine fields and even metal-rich deposits may exist beneath the sea.

Mineral resources of the seabed

When molten igneous rocks are extruded on the sea floor, a number of reactions occur. It has been discovered, for example, that if the lava is rather viscous, extensive physical and chemical reactions between the hot lava and the cold sea water result in the lava being shattered and pulverized. It has also been demonstrated that, as we might expect, the surface of the lava is rapidly chilled but that because rock is a poor conductor of heat, the interior portions cool very slowly.

During the slow cooling process, certain elements, such as iron, manganese, cobalt, copper, gallium, and lead, are selectively leached from the interiors of the rock masses and solubilized in the hot sea water. The metal-bearing exhalations are apparently soon cooled; the iron in solution is oxidized and deposited as a fine-grained or even colloidal sedimentary blanket of iron oxides. As the colloidal precipitate settles, it carries with it much of the copper, lead, manganese, and other elements leached from the volcanic rocks. Copper and lead contents of up to 2,000 parts per million have been reported, for example.

Several such metal-rich sedimentary layers have been encountered during deep-sea dredging and drilling operations along the oceanic ridge system in both the Atlantic and Pacific oceans. On one cruise in the South Atlantic, for example, scientists on the Deep-Sea Drilling Project encountered a layer about 6 meters thick consisting entirely of amorphous iron oxide. Older sediments have also been discovered away from the present spreading centers, suggesting that these layers may be common features associated with underwater volcanism and that they are therefore widely distributed on the continually spreading deep ocean floor.

The iron-rich sediments discovered to date have not proved to have contents of copper, lead, zinc, and other desirable metals sufficiently high to warrant recovery or even to reach the high values found in the Red Sea sediments. The fact that the process occurs at all, however, indicates that a potentially effective concentration mechanism exists and that continued ocean explorations may well reveal a sediment with interesting metal contents.

Resources from the Deep Ocean Floor: Manganese Nodules

The deep oceans have rather featureless bottoms compared to the topographic diversity observed along the oceanic ridges and continental margins. We have seen that the rocks underlying the deep oceans are basalts

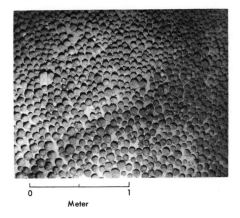

FIGURE 4-17 *Photograph of the deep Pacific Ocean floor (36°36.8 S 149°00.2 W; 5320 meters deep) showing a field of ferromanganese nodules. (Courtesy of Lamont-Doherty Geophysical Observatory of Columbia University.)*

that formed at the midoceanic ridges but then moved away from the ridge by crustal spreading. As the slow movement proceeds, a cover of fine-grained sediments, amounting to several hundred meters in thickness, accumulates and covers the basalts. Any metallic deposits within the basalts will probably never be found through this cover, even if the technology to work them in the ocean deeps could be developed.

The main interest with the deep ocean, as far as resources are concerned, is centered on manganese nodules.

In many areas one of the prominent features of the ocean bottom is an abundance of rounded, blackish nodules composed chiefly of the hydrated oxides of iron and manganese (Fig. 4–17). The nodules commonly grow as coatings on shells of pelagic organisms preserved in the sediments. They vary in size from "micronodules" a millimeter or so in diameter which weigh less than one gram up to masses many centimeters in diameter weighing almost 400 kg. Most are between 1 and 20 cm in diameter.

The interest in manganese nodules as a potential resource lies not so much in their manganese contents but in the fact that many valuable metals are enriched in them. In addition to the approximately 23 percent manganese and 6 percent iron present in an average nodule, it may contain about 1 percent each of copper and nickel and slightly lesser quantities of cobalt. The prospect of recovering the copper and nickel from such a highly enriched potential resource has kindled the interest of a number of major companies in the world. Several have shown sufficient interest to invest in detailed exploratory programs.

The distribution and abundance of manganese nodules were estimated in the past by photographing the ocean floor, by the accidental trapping of the nodules in sediment cores or in deep dredge hauls, or by material balance calculations. Today, the exact limits of manganese nodule "fields" are being assayed by means of deep-sea television cameras.

Manganese nodules, although covering perhaps 25 percent of the ocean bottom, are not homogeneously distributed within the basins. A map of nodule abundance in the Pacific is shown in Fig. 4–18. Finer-scale distribution patterns have also been worked out now for potential sites for mining by using the television camera technique.

The compositions of the nodules also vary regionally. Figure 4–19 shows the distribution of nickel concentrations in manganese nodules in the Pacific. Clearly, one must consider the concentration of the desired metals, as well as the abundance of nodules, in evaluating the nodules as a potential.

The total manganese nodule resource of the oceans has recently been estimated to be about 6×10^{11} tons—a sizable potential resource if recovery and processing were economically feasible. The path to the economic exploitation of manganese nodules, however, has several important obstacles that must be overcome. First, a suitable area for manganese nodule recovery must be chosen on the basis of abundance of nodules, their compositions,

FIGURE 4-18   *The relative distribution of manganese nodules on the Pacific Ocean floor.*

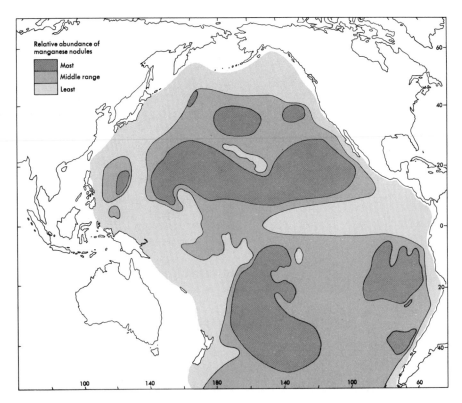

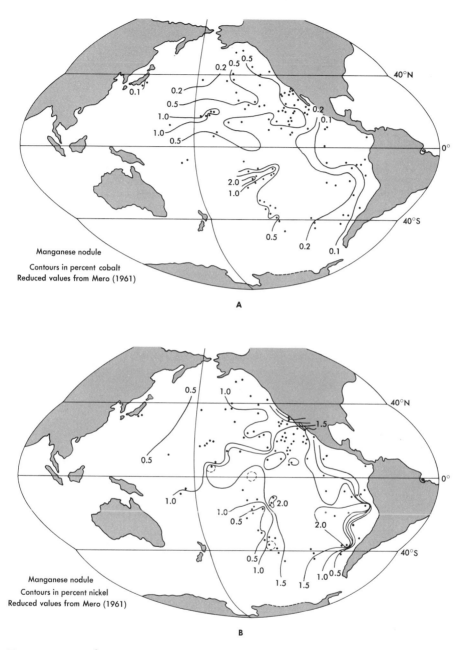

FIGURE 4-19 *The compositions of manganese nodules vary from place to place.*
The nodules always contain manganese and iron oxides, and it is in the minor
elements, such as cobalt and nickel, that the greatest variations show up. (A) The
cobalt content of nodules in the Pacific. (B) The nickel content. Values are given
in weight percent on a detrital mineral-free basis ("reduced") as given by J. L.
Mero, 1961, Mineral Resources of the Sea, *Elsevier Pub. Co.*

Mineral resources of the seabed

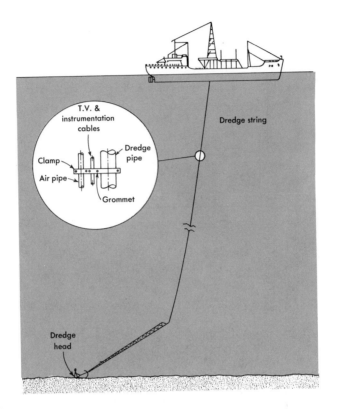

FIGURE 4-20 *The air-lift technique for collecting manganese nodules.*

and access to adequate staging areas. Next, a completely novel technology of mining is required by which the nodules can be transported as much as 6000 meters from the ocean bottom to the surface. Finally, an extractive metallurgy must be created specifically for the nodules, for all the desired metals are dispersed in an exceedingly fine-grained intergrowth of manganese minerals.

The identification of suitable sites for manganese nodule recovery can be done, as we have seen, by means of several exploratory techniques, the most refined of which is the underwater television camera. The chemical assay of nodules is a routine procedure. The major technical problems thus lie in the method of mining and the method of extracting the desired metals in a pure state from the complex manganese nodule material.

Two methods of mining nodules have been used successfully in pilot projects. One depends on a suction technique that uses forced air as a lifting agent (Fig. 4–20); the other uses a string of buckets dragged along the bottom and then recovered in a continuous chain fashion (Fig. 4–21).

In July 1970 the R/V (Research Vessel) *Deepsea Miner*, using the air-lift suction technique, first successfully recovered manganese nodules from a depth of 800 meters on the Blake Plateau off the southeastern coast of the United States. At about the same time, the Japanese ship *Chiyadu-Maru* began using the continuous bucket-line system in about the same depth of water off the Japanese coast. Subsequent tests at greater depths, up to about 4000 meters, by the Japanese have confirmed the potential of their system.

The Japanese group believes that, in a suitable site, they can recover about 40 tons a day of manganese nodules from a depth of 4000 meters. The air-lift method used by the American group (Deepsea Ventures, Inc.)

FIGURE 4-21   *An alternate device for recovering manganese nodules from the deep ocean floor. A string of buckets is lowered, dragged across the ocean floor, then brought back up with a load of nodules.*

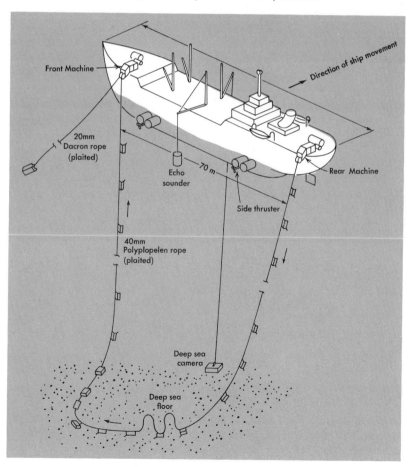

Mineral resources of the seabed

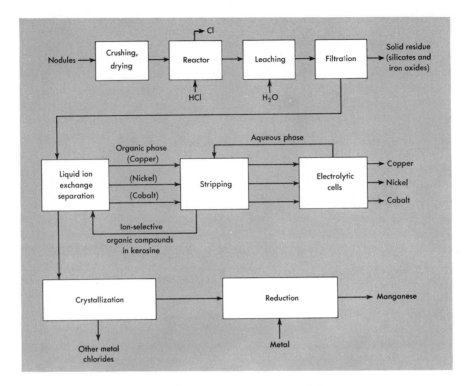

FIGURE 4-22 *A processing plan worked out by the Deepsea Ventures Company to recover manganese and other such metals as copper, nickel, and cobalt from manganese nodules.* After Chemical and Engineering News, *1971.*

is designed ultimately to recover about 1 to 2 million tons a year of manganese nodules for each operating dredge. Of course, these are both ideal goals that may not be met on a continuous operating basis.

The second major problem, once the ore is transported to a suitable site for unloading, is the extraction of the desired metals from the nodules. One pilot process being explored by Deepsea Ventures, Inc. is shown in Fig. 4–22. The process first involves the reduction of Mn^{+4} in the nodules to Mn^{+2}, using hydrogen chloride gas at 120°C. The result is the formation of chlorine gas and the conversion of all the metals under consideration for economic recovery into water-soluble chlorides. Leaching by water then extracts copper, nickel, cobalt, and manganese (and other metal) chlorides. These elements are subsequently isolated from each other by ion-exchange processes that are specific for each element in a continuous-flow process.

The future of manganese nodule exploitation for metals—in particular, copper and nickel—depends on many factors. Two important considerations are the long–term efficiencies of both the mining and the recovery processes. Another important factor may well prove to be ownership of minerals in international waters. Without full-scale testing, it is probable that none of these doubts can be completely answered.

Energy

The controlled release of energy to supplement human labors, together with the ability to readily convert one energy form to another, laid the foundations of the Western industrial civilization. As this civilization and the population it supports grow larger, we become daily more dependent on a continuing supply of inexpensive supplemental energy. Our future now depends on it, for it is only through the agency of cheap supplemental energy that we can conceivably provide a technological future for our ever-burgeoning, and city-centered, population. A controlled decrease in energy use, and with it a slow reduction in population, is possible but would still place such heavy demands on the total supplies of conventional energy sources, such as gas, oil and coal, that we are forced to question their adequacy to meet the demand. Supplemental energy supplies have become Western civilization's most vital resource, and the extension of the quest for them to the sea has become its most recent preoccupation.

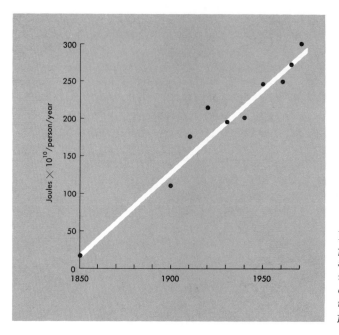

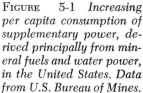

FIGURE 5-1 *Increasing per capita consumption of supplementary power, derived principally from mineral fuels and water power, in the United States. Data from U.S. Bureau of Mines.*

Man's Use of Energy

Domesticated animals as beasts of burden and wood for burning were the earliest sources of supplemental energy for mankind. A turning point came in the twelfth century, when inhabitants on the northeast coast of England found that the inflammable black "sea coles" weathering out of coastal cliffs were suitable substitutes for their previous wood supplies. The usage spread rapidly, and by the latter half of the thirteenth century it was necessary to pass laws in an attempt to limit the obnoxious odors and air pollution arising from its burning. Finally, in 1306, King Edward I made the burning of coal a capital crime. Depletion of the great forests of England and Europe gave such a law little meaning, however, and the discovery that coke derived from coal could be substituted for charcoal in the smelting of iron resulted in a tremendous expansion in its usage. Air pollution became a problem of daily annoyance for Western man. With the invention of the steam engine by Watt, in 1769, a ready way to convert heat energy to mechanical energy was available, and the industrial society was born. The burning of coal as a heat source immediately started to spiral, and the seeds of our present population explosion were sown.

The rapid spread of industrialization, and the expansion of major communities into the colder regions of the world, where they followed the daily activity patterns of temperate-climate communities, resulted in a rapidly increasing per capita power consumption. The trend continues unabated today. The more industrialized the society, the faster the rate of growth. Highly industrialized societies, like the United States, where the population doubles approximately every 50 years, now double their supplementary power consumptions approximately every 13 years (Fig. 5–1).

Coal, of course, has not been the sole source of supplementary power. With the first commercial production of petroleum, in 1857 in Romania, followed 2 years later in the United States by the now famous wells in Pennsylvania, an even more powerful and easily handled fuel became available. The relative importance of coal has declined as a consequence and that of crude oil and natural gas has grown continuously (Fig. 5–2). So great have been these growths, both of total power consumed and of the amount of petroleum used, that widespread concern has been expressed for the adequacy of the petroleum and coal resources of the world to sustain even the present use rate, let alone an increasing rate. As we shall see, this concern is well founded.

FIGURE 5-2   *Total production of supplementary energy in the United States from different sources. Nuclear power production is still too small to be seen on such a plot. Data from U.S. Bureau of Mines.*

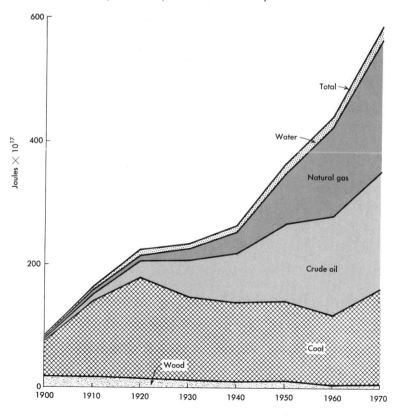

Units of Energy

Before discussing energy sources, it is necessary to define some units so that different energy sources can be directly compared. Energy appears in different forms; therefore we have a number of different units. The ones we shall use are the *calorie,* which is the amount of *heat energy* needed to raise the temperature of 1 gram of water by 1°C; the *erg,* which is the amount of *mechanical energy* used when a force capable of accelerating a 1 gram weight to a velocity of 1 centimeter per second in 1 second, is applied for a distance of 1 centimeter; and the *joule,* which is the *electrical energy* needed to maintain a current of 1 ampere for 1 second at a potential of 1 volt.

$$1 \text{ joule} = 0.2390 \text{ calorie} = 10,000,000 \text{ ergs}$$

The amount of energy available is an important figure, but another vital figure has a time connotation and is the rate at which energy is used. This time-dependent figure is called *power,* and its use is essential for our purposes because energy can only be used as fast as it becomes available:

$$\text{Power} = \frac{\text{energy}}{\text{time}}$$

Because electricity is increasingly becoming the form in which energy is produced and distributed, we shall use the common unit of electrical power, the watt, which is equal to a joule of energy being consumed every second. A watt is a small unit in terms of industrial-power consumption, however, so it is common to use a larger unit of 1000 watts, called a kilowatt. How much power is a kilowatt in everyday terms? It is enough to keep 10 light bulbs of 100–watt capacity burning or two electrical irons hot. It is also equivalent to 1.33 horsepower or the power we can get from ten able-bodied working men.

Sources of Energy

Energy reaches the Earth's surface from three different sources (Fig. 5–3). First, from the Sun we receive radiant energy, part of which is reflected directly back to space. The major part of the Sun's energy passes into or through the atmosphere and eventually flows through a number of paths, as shown in Fig. 5–3, whereby it controls such familiar processes as the rainfall cycle, wind, waves, and living matter. A small fraction of this solar-derived energy may be temporarily stored in water reservoirs and in living or fossil plants, but most of the energy eventually returns to space as very long wavelength heat waves. The second energy source is tidal, which is very much smaller than the solar radiant energy but, nevertheless, is a large power source. The third source is the geothermal energy flowing from the Earth, which, in turn, is derived both from the Earth's accumulated heat energy and from the heat generated within it by spontaneous nuclear decay of natural radioactive elements. Total geothermal energy, like the tidal source, is very small compared to the energy from incident solar radiation.

FIGURE 5-3   *The flux of energy at the Earth's surface is supplied from three sources: from the Sun, from the tides arising from the gravitational forces, and from the heat escaping from the Earth. Energy coming from the Sun is either reflected directly without change of wavelength or is absorbed and follows various paths before reradiated to space as long-wavelength radiation. The unit of energy is the joule. Because the energy flux is continuous, it is convenient to express it in watts, where one watt is equal to a joule per second. Solar radiation power of 17.3×10^{16} watts therefore supplies 1.5×10^{22} joules of energy to the Earth each day. The energy from ten days of sunlight on Earth is thus equivalent to the total energy stored in fossil fuels. Adapted from M. K. Hubbert, 1971,* Pub. 1000-D, National Academy of Sciences, *and* Scientific American, *v. 224, pp. 60–87.*

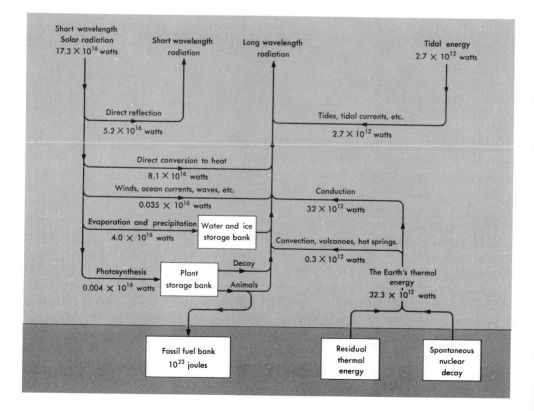

The energy flux is enormous. Whereas the total supplementary power now used *annually* by man falls between 10^{20} and 10^{21} joules, the amount of solar energy falling *daily* on the Earth is 1.5×10^{22} joules. Supplementary energy used by man has traditionally been produced from animals, plants, fossil plants, streams, river and lake waters, and winds, each of which depends directly on solar radiation as the prime source. Customarily, the most important of these sources have been contemporary plants and the accumulated debris of dead plant and animal matter, commonly called *fossil fuels*. With the adequacy of these sources now questioned, alternate energy supplies must be examined. The oceans are vitally important as potential energy sources, and they must be examined from two aspects—first, as direct-power suppliers and, second, as the harborers of fuels, such as petroleum, from which energy can be released at a controlled rate.

In comparison with the many potential mineral resources of the ocean basins discussed in Chapter 4, the present value of known and potential fossil fuel deposits is incomparably greater. Although fossil fuels is a term covering all fossilized forms of organic matter that might be used as fuel, the two forms that most concern us are crude oil, the liquid fraction of petroleum, and natural gas, the gaseous fraction.

The fossil fuels are produced as a by-product of the same photosynthesis process that maintains life on Earth. Life-forming materials will normally degrade to carbon dioxide and water. Natural plant decay is a slower degradation of plant matter than straight burning, but the same chemical processes are involved as in burning, and the end products, CO_2 and H_2O, are the same. As a matter of fact, to a first approximation, the contemporary rate of plant decay almost equals the rate of photosynthesis. The small difference represents the amount that is stored in sediments. There are a few favored environments where the decay process may be slowed down sufficiently for some of the organic debris to form local accumulations in sediments. These accumulations are converted by geological processes into deposits of petroleum, coal, oil shale, and other fossil fuels. During the 600 million years that plant and animal life have been abundant on Earth, these accumulations, although individually small in size and widely dispersed, have formed in aggregate a fossil fuel store that is now large by comparison with man's daily needs. It is clear, however, as depicted in Fig. 5–3, that the total energy available from fossil fuels is only a few hundred times greater than our current use rates and that in a long-term context mankind's reliance on fossil fuels can only be a transitory phase in history. We are now deeply immersed in the age of fossil fuels, however, and must look to further supplies of the same sort for many years to come. Among the potential fuel resources from ocean basins, crude oil and gas are the most abundant and the most important, and, therefore, will receive the most attention.

Petroleum

Origin and Distribution of Petroleum

Essentially all sediments contain some organic debris, of both plant and animal origin, and this debris is the precursor of the fossil fuel we call petroleum (from the Greek words for "rock" and "oil"). The large molecule hydrocarbon compounds of living plants and animals differ somewhat from those found in petroleum, and a complex, still little-understood series of changes are involved in the change. The conversion process apparently commences as soon as the organic debris is deposited, when bacteria and other small forms of animal life, which live off the organic debris, start passing it through their intestinal tracts and redeposit it in a partly degraded form as fecal matter. Further conversions occur spontaneously as the sediments are buried and consequently heated and subjected to higher pressures. At shallow depths, not only are the chemical rates very slow but the modification or destruction of the organic matter by ground waters also occurs. This process happens, in part, because of the role ground water plays in transporting oxygen and microorganisms downward (see Chapter 4 for the section on sulfur production in salt domes where a similar role for ground water is discussed). The petroleum-forming process is therefore effectively inactivated at shallow depths. Experience has shown that a sedimentary sequence must be greater than 800 meters below the surface to offer a reasonable probability for the discovery of significant oil or gas fields.

In the process of modification of deposited organic materials to form petroleum, the earliest compounds tend to have high molecular weights and they produce viscous, or "heavy" oils. With rising temperatures, the large molecules are broken down, or "cracked," into lighter and more mobile molecules, so that, in general, the longer the process continues, the "lighter" and more mobile the petroleum becomes. Although the diversity of organic molecules in petroleum is enormous and the types of molecules directly control the wide range of physical properties, such as color, volatility, and viscosity, that we observe, the bulk compositions of petroleums change very little (Table 5–1).

As sediments containing associated water and compounds antecedent to petroleum accumulate in a basin, the deeper parts are compacted under the weight of the added overlying material. Under pressure the porosity decreases, and the released water, and the petroleum that has been generated, are squeezed upward. Where barriers or impermeable traps are inter-

Table 5–1

Composition Range of Typical Crude Oils*
Compared to Average Compositions of Wood and Bituminous Coal†

Element	Crude Oil (%)	Wood (%)	Bituminous Coal (%)
Carbon	82.2–87.1	49.6	84.2
Hydrogen	11.7–14.7	6.2	5.6
Sulfur	0.1–1.5	Trace	1.0
Nitrogen	0.1–1.5	0.9	1.5
Oxygen	0.1–4.5	43.2	8.7

*After A. I. Levorsen, 1967, *Geology of Petroleum*, W. H. Freeman and Co.
†After F. W. Clark, *The Data of Geochemistry*.

posed in the path of the upward-migrating fluid, accumulations of petroleum may result: these sought-after concentrations are called "oil pools" or "gas pools."

Sediments of the Pliocene Epoch, deposited between 7 and 2.5 million years ago, contain, on the average, the highest ratio of trapped oil for a given rock volume; and the ratio decreases as we move backward in time, although not uniformly so, because some epochs produced larger percentages of petroleum-favorable rocks than others. Because erosive forces have had the shortest time to strip away the youngest sediments, it should hardly be surprising to learn that nearly 60 percent of all the oil discovered to date has been in sediments of the Cenozoic Era, covering only the last 10 percent of the time range in which petroliferous sediments are known to occur (Fig. 5–4).

Petroleum occurs in both ancient marine deposits and nonmarine deposits, but is considerably more abundant in the former. Although both ancient lake deposits and ocean deposits provided opportunities for the accumulation of organic material, the number of nonmarine sites of appreciable sediment thicknesses are rare compared to marine sediments. The search for petroleum around the world has therefore been most successful in the ancient sedimentary basins, and their extents on land have now been fairly clearly delineated (Fig. 5–5).

Experience has shown that no more than 2 percent of the area of the world's ancient sedimentary basins has a very high probability of yielding large petroleum production and that only 16 percent has a fair prospect of containing accumulations sufficiently large to warrant the expense of recovery of the remainder. For an additional 40 percent, prospects can only be rated marginal at best. For the remaining 42 percent, the probability of finding petroleum is essentially zero.

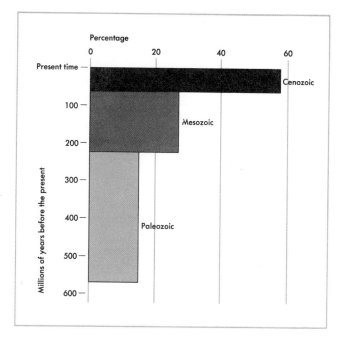

Percentage

FIGURE 5-4 *Estimated production of crude oil from rocks of different geological ages. After G. C. Gester, 1948.*

Petroleum Under the Ocean

How can we hope to evaluate and assess the petroleum resources beneath the sea if we cannot exactly assess those on the continents? Naturally, we shouldn't expect to do any better under water than we can on land, but we might hope to make an estimate that will at least establish the comparative size of the subsea petroleum resources compared to those on land.

First of all, we note that the thickness of sediments and the modes and rates of deposition on the major ocean ridges and on the deep ocean floor are generally unfavorable for the collection of vast quantities of organic material transformable into petroleum. Consequently, our major interest will lie in the continental margin. We noted in Chapter 2 that the continental margin may be divided into three parts—the shelf, the slope, and the rise. Although this division does not have meaning everywhere, it provides a reasonable basis for a discussion. What, then, are the prospects for petroleum in the continental shelf, the continental slope, and the continental rise?

The major subsea petroleum potential occurs in the continental shelves of the world. In some cases, such as the Gulf of Mexico and the Persian Gulf, major onshore producing regions simply continue out under water

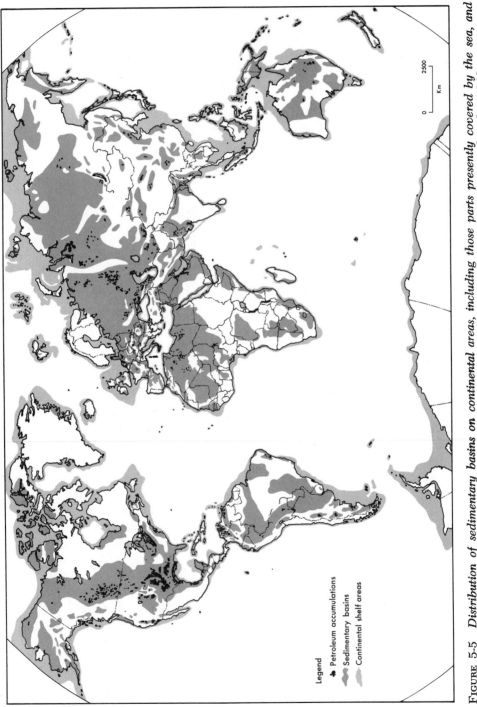

Figure 5-5 *Distribution of sedimentary basins on continental areas, including those parts presently covered by the sea, and the petroleum accumulations that have been discovered in them. After International Petroleum Encyclopedia, 1968.*

Legend

● Petroleum accumulations

Sedimentary basins

Continental shelf areas

0   2500
Km

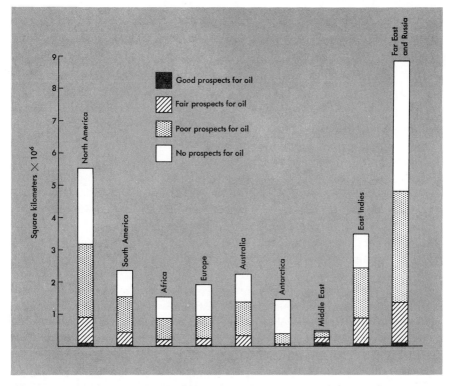

FIGURE 5-6 *Oil prospects of the continental shelves, in thousands of square kilometers. Adapted from the data of L. G. Weeks, 1965.*

and offer a maximum potential for oil discovery. In others, such as the oil and gas fields in Bass Strait off southern Australia, and in the North Sea between England and Holland, the entire section of petroleum strata is under water.

Where are the most promising shelf areas? North America, the Middle East, and the East Indies account for the great majority of the favorable regions (Fig. 5-6). In each case, much of the very promising land is adjacent to the onshore areas that are already highly productive. In North America, for example, the most favorable areas are in the Gulf of Mexico and the Arctic coast, although highly favorable areas also occur on the Atlantic and Pacific coasts. In the Middle East it is in the Persian Gulf, and in the East Indies it is around Sumatra and Borneo.

The continental shelf around the world, out to a depth of 330 meters, has an estimated area of about 28 million km². It is estimated that only 57 percent of the shelf is underlain by sediments of appreciable thickness in which petroleum accumulations may possibly occur. The remaining 43 percent is either metamorphic or igneous rock in which the petroleum potential is zero. Within the petroleum-favorable area, we might optimistically assess the chances for petroleum as being about the same as those on land. Thus about 2 percent, or 320,000 km², might be expected to fall in the most-favorable category, and some authorities believe that the actual potential might be higher because of a preponderance of young sediments on the shelves. The most optimistic evaluations only raise the figure of about 500,000 km². The search for offshore oil on shelves will therefore be as exacting and at least as risky as that on land.

Details of the continental slope are much less well known than details of the shelf, but those that are known suggest that the same types of petroleum-favorable rocks are to be found there. In many cases, sedimentary strata underlying the continental shelf are simply truncated by the continental slope (see Fig. 2–2), which thus becomes more of a geographic or topographic feature than a geologic one. Although exploration of the slope is still rudimentary at best, there is no obvious geological reason why its petroleum potential should be significantly different from that of the shelf. Because the rock types under the shelf and slope are very similar, and because there is no proven reason why water depth should change the petroleum potential, the most realistic estimate we can make is that their petroleum potentials are probably equally favorable. The slope has an areal extent of 27.4 million km², nearly the same as that of the continental shelf, which suggests that the two may possibly have the same long-term petroleum potential.

The most promising continental slope regions for major oil discoveries are less easy to pin down than their equivalents on the shelf. As a first approximation, it is a good bet that highly productive shelf regions will be matched by highly favorable adjacent slope regions. There may, however, be many isolated regions, such as the northeast coast of South America, where formerly shallow-water sediments are now found at water depths of 2000 meters or more, without an apparently continuous connection to equivalent sedimentary rocks in shallow water. One final promising site for subsea petroleum accumulations exists. At the boundary of the continent proper, which we have seen is the continental slope, we find a major zone of accumulating sediments. Transported by bottom currents, by slow creep down the slope under gravitational forces, and by turbidity currents along the submarine canyons cutting the slope, the wedge-shaped mass of sediments constituting the rise is the greatest single accumulation of erosional debris from continental weathering. The sediments that make up the continental rise are, in aggregate, the single largest mass of contemporary sediments of any type on Earth.

Several features suggest a very promising petroleum environment for the continental rise. Some are the direct consequence of the ocean floor spreading model in the new plate tectonic theory of the Earth's surface history, and others are related to the role of bottom transport in the oceans. As the Atlantic Basin began to open about 200 million years ago, for example, shallow-water sediments were formed, including, in part, marine evaporites. As separation continued, the shallow basins were ruptured, and the deposited sediments were draped over the continental edges of the moving plates. These sediments, formed in shallow waters, would now be found as part of the deep-water continental rise. In 1969 it was discovered that evaporite deposits buried beneath at least 1500 meters of later continental rise sediments off the Northern Coast of Africa have apparently given rise to salt dome-type structures in the continental rise (Fig. 5-7). Similar findings in the Gulf of Mexico were reported as far back as 1961 and were later confirmed by drilling aboard the *Glomar Challenger*. These structures could be sites of petroleum formation and concentration.

Despite these auspicious geological indicators, the occurrence of petroleum on the continental rise has not yet been clearly established. One very encouraging observation has been made, however. When a drill hole from the *Glomar Challenger* tested one of the Sigsbee Knolls in the Gulf of Mexico, petroleum indications were found in the drill cuttings recovered. Although not proven, therefore, the promise is excellent. How much petroleum might be there? It is impossible to make an estimate with any reasonable factual basis for accepting it. The best we can do is to use intuitive reasoning.

The areal extent of the continental rise is less than that of either the slope or the shelf, about 19.2 million km². It is not reasonable to assume that all of the rise might be in the highest petroleum potential category; we would probably have seen some external evidence, like escape of natural oil and gas to the surface, if this were the case. It can be argued however,

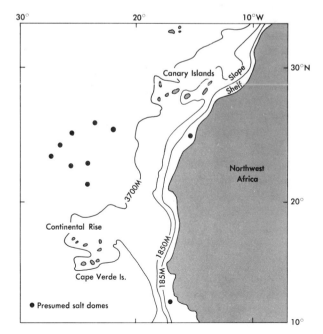

FIGURE 5-7 *Geophysical measurements across the wide continental rise off northwestern Africa have revealed what appear to be salt beds. Structures associated with salt domes often make ideal oil traps. After P. A. Rona, 1969, Science, v. 224, pp. 141–143.*

that all of the rise might be classified in the "fair prospect" category simply because we are dealing with young sediments. We might also argue that the rise should be treated like the slope and shelf, recognizing that volcanic debris and other unfavorable rocks for petroleum must contribute significantly to the sedimentary pile. Whichever assumption we make, the large areal extent underlain by rise sediments suggests that it must be considered a potentially important petroleum province and that, under optimistic circumstances, it might yield as much petroleum as either the shelf or the slope. Nevertheless, we must recognize that we may be overly optimistic with our estimates and that our intuitive geological arguments may well prove to be wrong.

Although we have identified the most likely areas in which future petroleum resources might be found, we have not offered a numerical estimate of exactly how much might be present and how much might be recovered. Many questions difficult to evaluate arise in making abundance estimates, and even on land there is a lack of agreement between authorities as to how much petroleum we may eventually recover. Most estimates for the ultimate potential of onshore deposits range between 1000 and 2000 billion barrels of oil. Offshore estimates generate even less accord. For example, it is observed that by carefully controlled withdrawal of crude oil from a reservoir on land as much as 35 percent of the crude oil present may be recovered. After initial withdrawal techniques have been completed, it is also found that an additional yield, of perhaps 10 percent, can often be obtained by various fracturing, flushing, and underground heating techniques. Although these techniques can be used on land, similar operations in deep water may not have the same success. Therefore estimates of such a straightforward factor as recovery efficiency are open to debate.

It is probable that the largest uncertainty underlying the estimate of subsea petroleum resources is the size of fields to expect. The effect of deposit size on the economics of production of any resource was discussed in Chapter 3. It is clear that only the largest oil and gas fields can be profitably sought and exploited at sea because of high equipment costs and the difficulties of working in deep water. The deeper the water, the greater the costs of searching for, and producing oil are likely to be.

The size of oil fields ranges from a few hundreds of thousand barrels to 20 billion barrels or more. Large fields are considerably less frequent than small ones, however. In the United States, for example, approximately 23,000 oil and gas fields have been discovered, but only 260 are so-called giant oil fields and will yield 100 million barrels of oil or more and only 47 are giant gas fields and will yield more than 1 trillion cubic feet of gas. Significantly, however, it is estimated that approximately 60 percent of the ultimate production of both oil and gas will come from such giant fields. It is not difficult to imagine how important the giant fields have been to the efficiency and profitability of the oil industry. They will be even more important, in fact, essential, for the economic production of deep offshore petroleum. It has been pointed out that only the giant fields can be profitably sought and produced in the deeper parts of the continental shelf and the slope. It has even been suggested that if we are ever to produce petroleum from the continental rise, even more stringent limitations might have to be met and that only fields capable of yielding a billion or more barrels of oil could be exploited.

Within limitations such as those just mentioned, optimistic evaluations of offshore petroleum potentials suggest that they may be about the same size as the onshore potential. Included in our use of the word potential are both past and future production. With available petroleum resources on land being rapidly depleted by heavy usage, exploitation of offshore resources must clearly grow larger with each passing year. Furthermore, if our guesses as to the offshore potential are correct, we can predict that within one or two decades we will see the day when offshore exceeds onshore production.

Energy from the Oceans' Waters

Energy resources specific to ocean water are centered in its tidal, current, and wave forces, in its temperature differences, and in the chemicals dissolved in it. Conceivably, each source might eventually be utilized, but at present only the tidal source is used on a large scale. Although wave energy is obviously massive and, in fact, exceeds tidal energy by many hundreds of times, the chances of harnessing it still seem to be small. There is a similarly small possibility that thermal energy may be usable under certain conditions; and no one has yet proposed a way to utilize the energy of major ocean currents. Each potential source of energy will therefore be briefly discussed, but our major interest will be centered on tidal power.

Tidal Power

Tides arise as a result of the lunar and solar gravitational interactions with Earth. Of the two, the effect of the Moon, because of its close proximity, dominates. The Sun's tidal attraction is only about half as large as the Moon's attraction. The major tidal cycles are, therefore, principally paced by the Moon, but the frequency is altered and the amplitude modulated by the complex interactions of the Earth-Moon-Sun system.

If we imagine the simplest form of interaction dominated by the Moon, it is a uniform tidal bulge passing around the Earth. Some energy is dissipated, however, primarily against the boundaries of the ocean basin, because of frictional resistance to the moving tidal bulge. The simple picture is complicated by the irregular shape of the Earth's surface. In the deep ocean basins, where tidal amplitudes rarely exceed a meter and where the ratio of bottom surface area to water volume is small, frictional losses of energy from the water interacting with the bottom are minimum. On the continental margins, however, especially where the water depth decreases rapidly, we observe that tidal amplitudes increase sharply, and frictional effects, being larger because of the increase in the ratio of basin bottom area to water volume, dissipate a proportionally large amount of energy.

The losses of energy by these tidal interactions actually decrease the force of attraction controlling the rotating Earth-Moon-Sun system. In particular, the effect is most marked in the Earth-Moon system, where the Moon's orbit is found to be slowly retreating from the Earth and, as a result, both the period of rotation of the Moon around the Earth and the period of rotation of the Earth about its axis are slowing down. The tidal motions are essentially acting as a giant brake. The Earth's period of rotation—that is, the length of the day—is lengthening at the rate of about 0.001 second per century. The changing length of the day can be measured, and from it the amount of tidal energy being dissipated can be calculated. This value is 2.7×10^{19} ergs of tidal energy, which are dissipated every second (2.7×10^{12} watts) in slowing the Earth-Moon system. Approximately one third of this amount is dissipated in the shallow seas, bays, and estuaries of the world, which collectively account for no more than 1 percent of the ocean surface. A large amount of the total tidal energy is thus concentrated in a very small fraction of the ocean near the continental coasts. Coastal regions are, of course, the most accessible portions of the ocean; consequently, they are potentially valuable sites for man to harness tidal energy.

This is hardly a new realization. Coastal dwellers have been using estuarine tidal waters to turn paddle wheels and drive pumps and mills for many centuries, particularly in regions with favorably high tidal amplitudes, such as the Breton coast of France and parts of Holland, Ireland, and England. The existence of tidal mills in England is even recorded in the Doomsday Book, a compilation of land ownership made in 1086 by order of William the Conqueror. European settlers brought knowledge of tidal mills with them to the New World, and many were installed along the eastern coast of North America. Boston, for example, had a tidal mill grinding corn as early as 1650.

With the development of electrical generators, the tidal energy that was used for so long as a source of mechanical energy could finally be converted to an energy form capable of the wide distribution that is characteristic of modern energy utilization. The method of producing tidal hydroelectric energy is essentially the same as that used in hydroelectric plants on rivers—water flows from one height to a lower one and turns a turbine as it does so. There is, of course, a difference in that with tides there is a two-way water flow and a short periodicity with which the head of water is established, whereas stream flow, properly regulated by a dam system, is unidirectional and constant. These differences cause great practical difficulties, and the development of large-scale tidal exploitation has been hindered as a result.

The technical problems are being attacked, and many have been successfully solved, at the present time in at least two locations, the Rance Estuary in Brittany and Kislaya Bay near Murmansk in the U.S.S.R. The question is clearly not of technical feasibility but rather of economics, and here we encounter three paramount limitations that must be evaluated.

The first limitation is imposed by the cost of manufacture of the water-driven turbines, the size of which must be inversely proportional to the head of water available to drive them. This relationship arises because the lower the head of water, the larger the volume required to produce a given amount of power and, therefore, the larger the turbine. The highest tides in the world have amplitudes of about 15 meters. If the water in a coastal basin is dammed at high tide and prevented from returning to the sea as the tide recedes, we could in theory, have a maximum of a 15-meter head of water at low tide with which to generate electricity. Even a 15-meter head of water is small by comparison with water heads developed in stream hydroelectric plants that commonly reach a hundred meters or more. Advanced technology has now produced large turbines that can operate in

FIGURE 5-8 *World sites with tidal ranges in excess of 5 meters, the only places where development of tidal power is feasible. The only places where tidal power is now being either exploited or tested are on the northwest coast of France, at the mouth of the River Rance, and in the White Sea.*

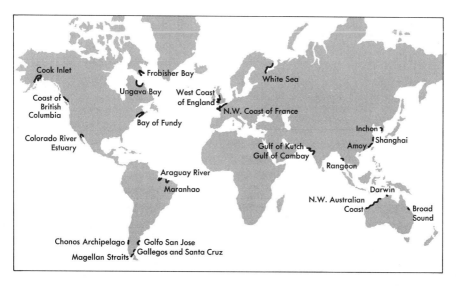

both directions as the tide flows both in and out. Double-acting turbines that can operate on water heads as low as a meter have also been produced, but because the basic efficiency of a turbine decreases as the water head decreases, the practical lower limit for water heads appears to be about 5 meters. The normal coastal tide is only about 2 meters, and the head of water possible in a tidal power plant under such circumstances is too small to be practical. Sites with suitably large tidal amplitudes are limited to a few regions of the world, and some are quite remote from present population centers or industries that might use the energy (Fig. 5–8).

The second limitation is imposed by the local topography of the potential site. Granted a suitably high tidal amplitude and accessibility to a population center, we must still face construction costs for the impounding dams. The longer and more exposed the mouth of the tidal bay or estuary, the higher the cost of dam construction. The ratio of dam length to volume of water impounded is, of course, the essential figure, and in this respect the dam on the Rance Estuary (Fig. 5–9) occupies one of the most favorable sites known.

Finally, there is the limitation that power production is controlled by the semidiurnal tidal cycle, and times of peak energy production thus necessarily change from day to day. Although the time of peak energy production is predictable from tidal charts, it is not easily controllable. If a large electrical network exists in the area, this disadvantage can be reduced by feeding the power produced into the network and matching the tidal electrical production against more easily regulated fossil fuel or nuclear power plants. The disadvantage can be still further reduced by using the tidal dams as an energy storage. The double-acting turbines can also be operated backward as pumps, so that water can be pumped into a dam when demand for power in the network is low, then run back to generate power at peak demand periods. If the pumping is done near high tide when the head of water is low, and recovered when the tide is down and the head high, more energy can be recovered than was used in the pumping. However, such solutions are clearly not practicable in sparsely populated regions of the world or where energy production is not already large.

Use of dual basins, in which one serves as a reservoir and the other as a catchment, allows more continuous power production and reduces the sharp periodicity of a single basin system. Unfortunately, suitable sites for paired basins are not abundant, and the luxury of continuous power must pay a penalty in reduced total energy recovered. The most likely use of tidal power in the future will thus be as an addition to diversified source power networks, and any utilization must continue to depend directly on the competitive cost of power produced from alternate sources. Unfortunately, even in the highly favorable Rance Estuary, it is not yet clear that power can or will be produced less expensively than it can be from other sources.

With these limitations, the sites around the world that are potentially sources for tidal power can be easily identified. The most important sites are around the Bay of Fundy, along the Channel coast of France, some of the British river estuaries, the White Sea coast of the U.S.S.R., the Golfo San Jose in Argentina, and the Kimberly coast in Australia. These sites

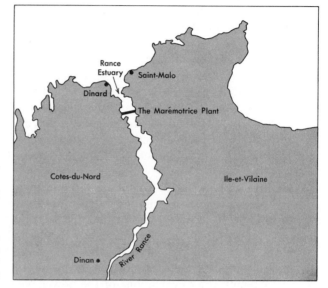

FIGURE 5-9 *Dam being constructed across the River Rance in France, used to regulate water flow during the diurnal tidal cycles. Town in the upper portion of the photograph is Dinard. (Photograph courtesy of Government of France.)*

account for 0.160×10^{12} watts, or only 16 percent of the tidal energy dissipated in shallow seas. Allowing a liberal 20 percent conversion rate to electrical power, man might feasibly recover 0.032×10^{12} watts of tidal hydroelectric power if all the sites were developed—barely more than 1 percent of the hydroelectric potential of 3×10^{12} watts estimated to be available in the world's rivers, most of which remains to be developed. Furthermore, over 50 percent of the estimated potential is centered on one of the world's least-hospitable and least-inhabited regions, the Kimberly coast of northwestern Australia.

Clearly, tidal power on a global scale can never be very important. Locally it may well assume major importance. The Rance Estuary tidal power project, using 24 turbines of advanced design operating on reversible flows, started in 1966 to produce 544,000 kilowatt-hours (1.96×10^{12} joules) of energy annually, which is 18 percent of the calculated potential available at the site. This is the only full-scale operation in existence at the present time. The only other operating tidal plant is in the small inlet, Kislaya Bay on the Barents Sea, where Russian engineers have installed a small pilot plant. The Bay of Fundy, which boasts the world's highest tides, also has a very large power potential, and numerous sites both in Canada and Maine have been carefully scrutinized for more than 40 years. During the middle 1930s a start was made by U.S. Army engineers to install a large tidal power scheme in Passamaquoddy Bay near the United States-Canadian border. After one year of work, the U.S. Congress withdrew further funds and all attempts to reactivate the scheme have proven unsuccessful.

In 1969 further evaluations of the power potential of the Bay of Fundy region were completed by both Canadian and United States government sources. Although technically feasible, power could not be produced competitively with that from fossil fuel sources. The most critical cost analysis was made by the two Canadian provinces, Nova Scotia and New Brunswick, whose shores bound the Bay of Fundy. They estimated that installation of single–flow turbines could produce power for 0.56 cent a kilowatt-hour but that double turbines, despite their ability to produce more power, could only produce it for 1.04 cents a kilowatt-hour. Energy produced from fossil fuel plants in the region at the same time was about 0.3 cent a kilowatt-hour, and costs projected for new fossil fuel plants were only 0.45 cent. The tidal plant was clearly not competitive unless additional major advantages would accrue, such as a massive reduction in air pollution or reduced transportation costs in the region by having a safe roadway across the Bay. These points are still being debated.

Thermal Energy

Referring to Chapter 2, we note that the ocean behaves as a huge heat engine through its complex circulation. Although it is impossible to extract heat energy directly from this great heat reservoir, it is possible to use the temperature difference between the bottom and surface waters for the transfer of heat that can be usefully harnessed. Surface-water temperatures in the Tropics are 25°C or higher, while near-bottom temperatures are consistently below 5°C. Just as the flow of water from one height to another can be used to generate electrical power, so can the analogous flow of heat from a hot body to a cool one be used for the same purpose.

Soon after the discovery of the vertical temperature gradient in the ocean, it was suggested that this temperature difference could be used as a power source. The first attempt to do just that was made by a French engineer in 1928 near Liège in Belgium. The success of the Liège experiment led, eventually, to a much more ambitious scheme tried near Abidjan on the West African Coast after World War II. Cold sea water from depth was pumped to the surface and used in the condensor of a turbine whose "steam" source was the vapor from warm lagoon waters heated by the Sun. The Abidjan installation was an economic failure, partly because sea water itself was used as the heat transport medium and partly because of poor choices in the selection of materials for the turbine housing, but it did establish beyond doubt the feasibility of the scheme.

New techniques of heat exchange using propane as a low-cost, non-corrosive heat transport medium, circulating inside huge flat-plate heat exchangers suspended from large floating platforms, have been suggested to extend the Abidjan experiment. Although no operating scale pilot plants have yet been built, it has been estimated that by such methods, electrical power could presently be generated from tropical seas, such as the Caribbean, at a price that compares favorably with power developed from more conventional sources. We will describe in Chapter 6 an experiment in which this power source is used to produce fresh water and chilled, dehumidified air.

There are many practical difficulties to such a scheme on a large scale, of course, such as how to move electrical power from sites far out in the ocean to continental users. Perhaps the most promising possibility for thermal energy is in tropical islands, sites where deep cold waters are close to shore and where conventional fossil fuel power sources are generally imported.

Chemical Energy

Sea water is an electrolyte solution and as such can, in theory, be used as a battery fluid, allowing chemical energy to be converted to electrical energy. Test models of a small sea-water battery have been made and run successfully for several years, but they have a practical drawback in that only a small amount of power can be produced per unit weight of battery. One constructed by Lockheed Electronic Co., for example, is reported to have yielded only 80 watt-hours per pound.

Table 5–2

Calculated Power per Meter of Wavefront
for Waves of Various Heights in a Water Depth of 9 Meters*

Wave Height	Wavelength	Power per Meter
0.6 meters	20 meters	0.9 kilowatts
1.8 meters	38 meters	10.1 kilowatts
3.0 meters	57 meters	30.9 kilowatts

*Adapted from L. Smith, Bureau of Engineering, U.S. Navy, Washington, D.C.

Although technical development of the sea-water batteries may well increase their efficiency and convenience, it seems unlikely that we shall ever use sea water as a major source of chemical energy.

Wave Energy

The total amount of energy in waves is many thousands of times greater than that in tides. This statement should not be surprising when it is realized that a wave 1.8 meters high passing in water 9 meters deep has approximately 10 kilowatts of power in each meter of wavefront. The calculated power in waves of several heights, assuming an average wavelength, is given in Table 5–2.

Wave power has been used to excite air columns and ring bells or whistles as navigational aids for many years, but only recently has serious attention been paid to the possibilities of recovering the energy on a large scale. Even though the possibilities do not seem too encouraging, some patents have already been granted. One scheme, patented by the Power Systems Company, proposes the use of troughs covered with a flexible film and filled with a hydraulic fluid. When placed on the sea floor, the weight of a passing wave forces the hydraulic fluid through a network of pipes and into a motor, which, in turn, drives a generator.

Other Energy Sources in the Ocean

Although possibilities of use seem vanishingly small at present, the ocean does contain two readily identified potential energy sources of enormous magnitude. The first lies in the energy of the major ocean currents. The Gulf Stream, for example, could yield an estimated 7×10^{21} joules of energy per year, an amount far greater than the total annual supplementary power used by mankind today. How this energy could ever be tapped remains in the realm of distant speculation.

The second huge potential energy source lies in the possibility for the development of energy from nuclear fusion. This is the process that takes place in an uncontrolled fashion in the hydrogen bomb, where the fusion of two or more atoms of light elements, produces a heavier element plus the emission of a great deal of energy. The greatest amount of energy possible comes from fusion of the lightest element, hydrogen, a reaction that produces most of the energy emitted by the Sun. Similar reactions involving heavier elements produce lesser yields of energy as the masses increase, but, on the other hand, they are easier to trigger and are probably also easier to control. The main reaction that has been produced in the hydrogen bomb, for example, involves the fusion of the two atoms of deuterium, a heavy isotope of hydrogen, to form helium. If this reaction could be carried out in a controlled fashion, we would have a near-limitless source of energy for the future. Each time two deuterium atoms combine to form a helium atom they release 7.9×10^{-13} joules of energy. Because each cubic centimeter of sea water contains an average of 10^{16} atoms of deuterium, we could potentially recover 7.9×10^3 joules per cubic centimeter. The volume of the ocean is 1.35×10^{24}cc, so the energy potential from deuterium alone is 10.7×10^{27} joules—sufficient at mankind's present energy use rate for ten million years.

Although hydrogen fusion has not been achieved, the process does occur in the Sun and may eventually be achieved in a controlled fashion on Earth. Because sea water is the major source of the Earth's hydrogen, it follows that it would also be the ultimate energy source if the necessary technological breakthrough were achieved. Considering that more energy is released by hydrogen fusion than by the equivalent deuterium reaction and that the abundance ratio of deuterium to hydrogen in the ocean is about 1 to 6500, it is clear that the potential energy from hydrogen fusion power reaches astronomically large numbers. It is also clear, from both the deuterium and hydrogen potentials, why so many authorities believe that nuclear fusion power is the only real solution for long-term, stable supplies of supplementary energy.

Much of the petroleum consumed is burned in internal combustion engines and is a major source of pollution. Desire for improved environmental quality means either the exhaust from engines must be controlled or neutralized, or a new cleaner fuel must be found. The cleanest, most powerful, and most efficient fuel available is hydrogen. Its only waste product is water. The easiest way to produce hydrogen is by electrolysis of sea water. Although the cost of the electrolytic production is high, it may be balanced by the decrease in the cost of anti-pollution devices.

6

The chemical resources of sea water

The ocean is not only the major repository of water on the Earth's surface, it is also a salt solution made up of all the chemical elements in varying concentrations. As is evident from Table 2–1, ten elements make up most of the dissolved salts in sea water. The remainder of the chemical elements are present in much lower concentrations, many of them at levels of fractions of parts per billion (Table 6–1). The history of attempts at economic exploitation of the dissolved components of sea water can be reasonably divided into the concentrated elements and the trace elements.

Trace Elements from Sea Water

Before the refined analytical work on the trace-element composition of sea water during this century, it was possible to think of ocean water as a repository for a large number of useful elements brought to it by the rivers of the world as a result of rock weathering. Many elements would be expected to accumulate in sea water. For example, the solubilities of silver, gold, mercury, and lead are very high in a high chloride concentration solution such as sea water, because of the formation of very soluble chloride complexes. The few analyses of sea water that were available tended to support this point of view many years ago.

This belief was transformed into action after World War I in Germany by Fritz Haber, the discoverer of the method for the cheap production of ammonia, who hoped to use the silver and gold extracted from sea water to help relieve the problem of the German war reparations. His experiments showed that gold could be economically extracted from sea water if it occurred at a concentration level of one part per billion, the level reported by some earlier chemists. This concentration of gold would represent a total oceanic gold reservoir of 10^{15} grams!

When Haber actually tried to extract gold and silver from sea water, however, he was completely frustrated because, as he later discovered himself, the actual concentration is not one part per billion but five to ten parts per *thousand* billion (Table 6-1), a hopelessly low concentration for profitable recovery!

Haber's experience, nevertheless, made urgent the question of what factors control the concentration levels of trace elements in the oceans. The oceans apparently are not behaving as a simple repository for metals transported from the continents over the 4.5 billion years of the Earth's existence.

Chemical Constraints on Concentration Levels

Knowing the general properties of sea water—its major elements, its saltiness, its acidity, and its oxidation state—we can estimate the solubilities of many of the metallic elements in sea water by assessing the highest expected concentration permitted by the least-soluble compound that might exist in the oceans (Table 6-2). (Metallic elements in solution generally exist as atoms that have lost electrons and are called ions.) The observed concentrations of most metals are considerably lower than those predicted by the solubility data and by the measured supply rate of streams. Of the few elements that are close to their expected concentrations, thorium and the rare-earth elements (lanthanum, cerium, etc.) appear to have their concentrations mainly controlled by the phosphate level of sea water because they form highly insoluble phosphate compounds. Manganese, iron, and aluminum are also close to their expected concentrations because of the highly insoluble oxides they form in sea water.

Although many of the metals exist in sea water as simple, positively charged ions surrounded by halos of water molecules, the ions of some metals form highly soluble and extremely strong chemical bonds with the negatively charged chlorine ions in sea water. These ions are called "complexes" and are very stable in solution. They thus increase the solubility of

Table 6–1

Composition of Streams and the Ocean

Atomic Number	Element	Sea Water (μg/liter)	Streams (μg/liter)
1	hydrogen	1.10×10^8	1.10×10^8
2	helium	0.0072	a
3	lithium	170	3
4	beryllium	0.0006	a
5	boron	4450	10
6	carbon (inorganic)	28,000	11,500
	(dissolved organic)	500	a
7	nitrogen (dissolved N_2)	15,000	a
	(as NO_3^{-1}, NO_2^{-1}, NH_4^{+1} and dissolved organic)	670	226
8	oxygen (dissolved O_2)	6000	a
	(as H_2O)	8.83×10^8	8.83×10^8
9	fluorine	1300	100
10	neon	0.120	a
11	sodium	1.08×10^7	6300
12	magnesium	1.29×10^6	4100
13	aluminum	1	400
14	silicon	0–2900	6100
15	phosphorus	0–88	20
16	sulfur	9.04×10^5	5600
17	chlorine	1.94×10^7	7800
18	argon	450	a
19	potassium	3.92×10^5	2300
20	calcium	4.11×10^5	15,000
21	scandium	0.0004	0.004
22	titanium	1	3
23	vanadium	1.9	0.9
24	chromium	0.2	1
25	manganese	1.9	7
26	iron	3.4	670
27	cobalt	0.05	0.1
28	nickel	2	0.3
29	copper	2	7
30	zinc	2	20
31	gallium	0.03	0.09
32	germanium	0.06	a
33	arsenic	2.6	2
34	selenium	0.090	0.2
35	bromine	67,300	20
36	krypton	0.21	a
37	rubidium	120	1
38	strontium	8100	70
39	yttrium	0.013	0.07
40	zirconium	0.026	a
41	niobium	0.015	a
42	molybdenum	10	0.6

The chemical resources of sea water

Table 6-1 (con't)

Number Atomic	Element	Sea water (μg/liter)	Streams (μg/liter)
43	technetium	(not naturally occurring)	
44	ruthenium	0.0007	a
45	rhodium	a	a
46	palladium	a	a
47	silver	0.28	0.3
48	cadmium	0.11	a
49	indium	a	a
50	tin	0.81	a
51	antimony	0.33	2
52	tellurium	a	a
53	iodine	64	7
54	xenon	0.47	a
55	cesium	0.30	0.02
56	barium	20	20
57	lanthanum	0.0034	0.2
58	cerium	0.0012	(0.06)
59	praseodymium	0.00064	0.03
60	neodymium	0.0028	0.2
61	promethium	(not naturally occurring)	
62	samarium	0.00045	0.03
63	europium	0.000130	0.007
64	gadolinium	0.00070	0.04
65	terbium	0.00014	0.008
66	dysprosium	0.00091	0.05
67	holmium	0.00022	0.01
68	erbium	0.00087	0.05
69	thulium	0.00017	0.009
70	ytterbium	0.00082	0.05
71	lutetium	0.00015	0.008
72	hafnium	<0.008	a
73	tantalum	<0.0025	a
74	tungsten	<0.001	0.03
75	rhenium	0.0084	a
76	osmium	a	a
77	iridium	a	a
78	platinum	a	a
79	gold	0.011	0.002
80	mercury	0.15	0.07
81	thallium	<0.01	a
82	lead	0.03	3
83	bismuth	0.02	a
84–89 and 91	(thorium and uranium decay series elements: polonium, astatine, radon, francium, radium, actinium, and protactinium)		
90	thorium	<0.0005	0.1
92	uranium	3.3	0.3

aNo data or reasonable estimates available.

The chemical resources of sea water

Table 6–2

Expected Equilibrium Concentrations for Some Elements and Complexes, Based on Insoluble Salts of Phosphate, Carbonate, Hydroxide, Sulfide, and Chloride*

(concentrations in log moles/liter)[a]

Element or Complex	PO_4^{-3} (log a = —9.3)	CO_3^{-2} (log a = —5.3)	OH^- (log a = —6)	S^{-2} (log a = —9)	Chloride Complex	Observed Titer Conc. in Sea Water
La^{+3}	—11.1	–	–	–	–	—10.7
Ce^{+3}	—10.0	–	–	–	–	—10.2
Th^{+4}	—11.8	–	–	–	–	—11.7
Cr^{+3}	—11.3	–	–	–	–	—8.0[b]
UO_2^{+2}	—9.2	–	–	–	–	—7.8[c]
Fe^{+3}	—10.6	–	–	–	–	—7.3[d]
Fe^{+2}	–	–	–	—6.4	–	—7.3[d]
Mn^{+2}	–	—3.1	+0.2	—2.6	–	—7.4
Co^{+2}	—4.4	—6.5	—2.2	—12.1	–	—8.2
Ni^{+2}	—2.9	—0.6	—3.2	—10.7	–	—6.9
Cu^{+2}	—5.1	—3.5	—5.8	—26.0	–	—7.3
Ag^{+1}	—2.0	—2.7	—1.5	—19.8	–	—8.5[e]
$AgCl_2^-$	–	–	–	–	—4.2	
Zn^{+2}	—3.5	—3.7	—3.5	—14.1	–	—6.8
Cd^{+2}	—3.7	—5.0	—0.5	—16.2	–	—9.0
Hg^{+2}	–	–	—12.5	—43.7	–	—9.1[e]
$HgCl_4^-$	–	–	–	–	+1.9	
$HgCl_2^0$	–	–	–	–	—0.3	
Al^{+3}	–	–	—12.0	–	–	—8.3
Ga^{+3}	–	–	—16.0	–	–	—9.3
Sn^{+2}	–	–	—15.0	—16.0	–	—8.2
Pb^{+2}	—6.8	—6.8	—2.0	—16.6	–	—9.8[e]
$PbCl_3^-$	–	–	–	–	—5.6	
$PbCl^+$	–	–	–	–	—5.8	

[a]Calculations made with the following activity coefficients: monovalent ions, 0.7; divalent ions, 0.1; trivalent ions, 0.01.

[b]Occurs primarily as CrO_4^{-2}.

[c]Occurs primarily as $UO_2(CO_3)_3^{-4}$.

[d]May occur as particulate phases.

[e]Occurs primarily as chloride complexes.

*After E. D. Goldberg, W. S. Broecker, M. G. Gross, and K. K. Turekian, 1971, *Radioactivity in the Marine Environment*, National Academy of Sciences, Washington.

these metals by competing with the insoluble compounds the metals might form. Another type of enhancement of solubility is seen in the case of uranium, which forms a highly soluble complex with the carbonate present in sea water. In addition, chromium and molybdenum form very soluble chromate and molybdate ions in normal sea water.

The chemical resources of sea water

Other Processes Controlling Trace-Element Concentrations in Sea Water

If the oceans do not contain most of the trace elements at saturation concentrations or even at the high values projected by stream supply rates, what other mechanisms of control can be invoked? Several have been suggested. They are (a) adsorption on suspended particles of clays and other materials, (b) biological removal, and (c) the chemical effect of near-shore and other anoxic (or oxygen-free) sedimentary environments.

Fine-grained sediments of the type reaching the ocean floor (mainly clays) can be shown to be ideal materials for the removal of certain elements by adsorption. Despite this fact, the role played by adsorption of trace elements on clays in the sea is probably of little importance in lowering the concentrations of the trace elements. The reason can be seen when we trace the history of a clay particle derived from the land. The particle, produced by weathering and erosion, has been in intimate contact with fresh waters during the weathering process or during stream transport. Adsorption of trace elements from such a dilute solution is expected to be high, and experiments in the laboratory simulating clay particles in streams verify this expectation, as does the experience from nuclear reactors, where cooling water spiked with radioactive tracers is in contact with stream sediments downstream from the reactor. However, when these particles encounter sea water, the tendency is to *release* the trace elements that were adsorbed rather than to adsorb more trace elements. The reason for this tendency is the massive competition for adsorption sites by the major elements in sea water, such as sodium, magnesium, potassium, and calcium. Therefore we find that particles brought to the oceans actually release trace elements rather than adsorb them.

Biological removal has often been invoked for the mechanism of modifying the trace-element composition of sea water. The argument is based on the trace-element analyses of marine organisms, which show that many have high trace-element contents relative to sea water (Table 6–3). An expectably high degree of concentration of phosphorus by organisms is found, for organisms require this element for all their life functions, including growth and reproduction. Table 6–3 shows that trace-element enrichment in organisms is considerably less than phosphorus enrichment.

Most of the phosphorus and trace elements extracted from the sea by organisms in the deep ocean are returned to the sea by degradation and oxidation processes occurring down the food chain of the oceans. In the case of anoxic sea water environments, like those in some fjords, the deep parts of the Black Sea, and the deep parts of some oceanic regions of intense upwelling and high surface biological productivity, the flood of organic debris falling from the surface is more than enough to use up the

Table 6-3

Concentration Factors between Sea Water and Plankton Ash for Some Trace Elements*

Element	Sea Water (μg/liter)	Plankton Ash (μg/g)		Concentration Factors (liters sea water per grams plankton ash)	
		Plants (Sargassum)	Animals	Plants (Sargassum)	Animals
P	0–88	20,000	20,000	≧230	≧230
Ag	0.3	0.3	0.3	1	1
Al	1	65	300	65	300
B	4450	1,200	140	0.27	0.031
Ba	20	120	52	6.0	2.5
Cd	0.11	8	13	72	120
Co	0.05	3	3	60	60
Cr	0.2	9	7	45	35
Cu	2	270	270	135	135
Li	170	6	40	0.04	0.2
Ni	2	27	12	14	6
Sr	8100	8,500	930	1	0.1
Ti	1	26	120	26	120

*After E. D. Goldberg, W. S. Broecker, M. G. Gross, and K. K. Turekian, 1971, *Radioactivity in the Marine Environment*, National Academy of Sciences, Washington.

oxygen supplied to the deep water by the local circulation mechanism. These anoxic waters are distinguished by a virtual absence of fishes. The rain of organic debris, however, does get partially utilized under anoxic marine conditions by sulfate-reducing bacteria with the consequent production of hydrogen sulfide (the typical rotten egg smell so often encountered in tidal mud flats).

Under the conditions of no oxygen and the high sulfide-ion concentration, the chemical characteristics of sea water are radically different from those in the much larger, aerated, open ocean environment. Where manganese and iron have low solubilities in oxygenated sea water, for example, the solubilities increase dramatically in anoxic environments. High concentrations of these elements are found in the deeper parts of the Black Sea (Fig. 6-1) and in anoxic fjords. Other metals, such as silver, mercury, and lead, decrease in their permissible concentrations because of the formation of highly insoluble sulfides, despite their capacity to form strong chloride complexes.

The sedimentary environments of hundreds of thousands of miles of estuarine areas of the world are quantitatively more important than the deep anoxic basins in modifying the trace-element composition of the open oceans. The waters of the estuarine environments normally are not themselves continuously anoxic, for the circulation is generally too rapid to deplete the oxygen in the water significantly under most conditions. Periodically, as in the case of the Baltic Sea, however, the inflow of oxygenated water is diminished, so that the deeper parts of the basin may become anoxic. Almost universally, the sediments underlying the water are very rich in organic material because of the high productivity of coastal areas and the short traverse of the debris to the bottom. This organic-rich mud bottom supports a rich fauna, including clams, lobsters, and worms. A few centimeters below the sediment-water interface, the dissolved interstitial oxygen is used up by these aerobic life forms and the sulfate-reducing anaerobic bacteria come into action. Most of the hydrogen sulfide, produced in the sediments, reacts with the ever-present iron oxide, derived mainly from weathered minerals, to form the iron sulfide minerals that give sediments from such environments their characteristic black color.

Trace metals, transported to the bottom of an estuarine basin by asso-

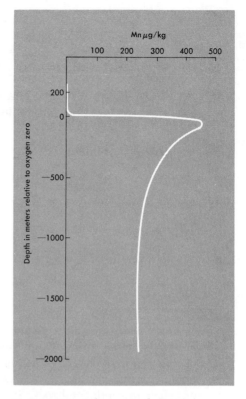

FIGURE 6-1 *The vertical distribution of dissolved manganese in the Black Sea. The high values at depth are due to anoxic conditions and the presence of dissolved hydrogen sulfide. After D. W. Spencer and P. G. Brewer, 1971, Jour. Geophys. Res., v. 76, pp. 5877–5892.*

ciation with falling organic debris, are released by decay of the organic matter into a reducing environment high in sulfide in concentration. Hence even the most soluble metals in an open sea water environment—silver, lead, and mercury, for example—are precipitated as highly insoluble sulfides and retained in the estuarine sediments.

The Potentials for Economic Exploitation of Trace Metals from Sea Water

At the present time, copper, lead, zinc, nickel, gold, uranium, and the other metals (excluding magnesium for the moment) are more efficiently recovered from land deposits than from sea water. This situation may change in the future, however, and it is important for us to assess the prospects of mining sea water for these elements when the only alternatives remaining on land are very lean deposits.

Table 6-4

Concentration of Rare Metals
in the Continental Crust and in Sea Water

Metal	Continental Crust (μg/gram)	Sea Water (μg/gram)
Chromium	48	0.0002
Manganese	670	0.0019
Cobalt	12	0.00005
Nickel	37	0.002
Copper	32	0.002
Zinc	63	0.002
Silver	0.06	0.00028
Tin	2.1	0.00081
Gold	0.002	0.000011
Uranium	2.9	0.0033

Every trace element is present in higher concentration in the continental crust than in sea water (Table 6-4). For example, the average concentration of uranium in rocks is 3 parts per million, whereas it is present at levels of only 3 parts per billion in sea water. Similarly, the average concentration of cobalt in continental rocks is 20 parts per million, whereas it is present in sea water at less than 50 parts per trillion. In addition, the average density of continental rocks is about three times the density of sea water, so that the concentration per volume instead of mass is proportionately greater in the rocks.

If we ever see the day when identifiable ore deposits no longer supply our needs, and we must turn to average rocks or sea water, the odds seem strongly in favor of rocks for most of the trace elements. The only advantage of using sea water as an ore is if the metal can be extracted at least one thousand times more efficiently from sea water solution than from solid rocks. At the moment, the likelihood of this does not seem to be great. A few acid-leaching experiments on rocks in the extraction of uranium, for instance, or the cyanide-complexing extraction of gold and silver indicates that it is possible to conceive of clever methods to extract metals from rocks even at low concentrations if necessary. Similar experiments of economic importance are generally lacking or have proven unsuccessful when sea water analogs are used. One such experiment that is worth discussing, however, is the study of uranium extraction from sea water.

The concentration of uranium in sea water is uniformly about 3 parts per billion. This is a relatively high concentration compared to the concentration of many trace metals in sea water. In the case of uranium, the high concentration can be directly attributed to the formation of a highly soluble complex species—the uranyl carbonate complex $UO_2(CO_3)_3^{-4}$. In the absence of carbon dioxide in the atmosphere, this complex would not form in sea water because the CO_3^{-2} species would be virtually eliminated and uranium by itself is quite insoluble in slightly basic sea water.

In order to recover uranium from sea water, a chemical extractant is required that will be highly effective under the salty, slightly basic state of sea water without itself being modified or dissolved in sea water. This limits our choice either to ion-exchange resins or to low-solubility compounds capable of efficiently reacting with the uranium in sea water without changing solubility. Most ion-exchange resins made from high polymer organic compounds generally do not meet these requirements. Titanium hydroxide coatings on glass, wool, or muslin or even as separate small granules ($\sim$ 0.1 cm diameter) would, however, do the job effectively. Titanium hydroxide is not only efficient as an extractant, it is also virtually insoluble in sea water and thus seems to be ideal for the task.

The reaction that takes place in sea water, resulting in the extraction of uranium is

$$Ti(OH)_4 + UO_2(CO_3)_3^{-4} \rightarrow Ti(OH)_2 \cdot O_2 \cdot UO_2 + CO_3^{-2} + 2HCO_3^{-1}$$

The uranium can be subsequently released by washing the coatings with acid.

One additional major requirement remains to be satisfied. Because the sea water solution is so dilute, a great deal of water must pass over the $Ti(OH)_4$ in order to extract a reasonable amount of uranium. The engineering requirements are, first, the construction of suitable highly permeable frames on which the titanium hydroxide granules or coated materials may be incorporated in order to interact with the flowing sea water. Second, these frames must be placed in an area of sufficiently rapid flow to ensure a continuous supply of new high-uranium sea water. Finally, the flow areas should be close to land for efficient monitoring.

Under the most ideal conditions, uranium extraction from sea water may be competitive with extraction from low-quality uranium ores on land. If a properly designed plant were set up in the Irish Sea at the Menai Straits to take advantage of the tidal currents there, uranium could be produced at 11 to 22 dollars per pound of U_3O_8. Although somewhat higher than the present costs from even low-grade uranium ore deposits, these figures may be competitive with more difficult extractions from shales or granite, both of which have been suggested as alternatives.

The known uranium reserves in ore deposits are more than adequate for the near future, assuming that use rates do not rise suddenly and drastically. However, if the demand for atomic fission power plants grows dramatically during the next two decades, as many observers believe it will, known supplies of rich uranium ores will not satisfy the demand. Under these

The chemical resources of sea water

Table 6–5

Annual Worldwide Production of Chemicals from Sea Water in 1968*

Chemical	Millions of Tons	Percent of Total Production
Sodium chloride	35	29
Bromine	0.102	70
Magnesium		
Metal	0.106	61
Compounds	0.690	6
Fresh water from desalination	142	59

*After W. F. McIlhenny, Dow Chemical Company.

circumstances, the extraction from sea water may be an important competitive option. Maritime countries with poor prospects for the discovery of suitable uranium deposits within their national boundaries may look more seriously at the oceans as a source for uranium for strategic purposes.

Major Elements from Sea Water

The major element resources from the sea have been, at various times, sodium and chlorine (as sodium chloride—"common salt"), bromine, and magnesium. Potassium has been obtained at times as a by-product in salt extraction, but it is of minor importance. Table 6–5 shows the annual worldwide production of these materials in 1968. Although the picture has remained virtually unchanged for salt, some marked changes have occurred since the beginning of the seventies in the sources of the other elements. These changes are due to the fact that chemicals from sea water must be competitive with resources on land in order to be economically desirable for exploitation. The major elements extractable from sea water are bulk items that must compete with supplies from other potential sources on the basis of comparative transportation and energy costs.

Since 1968 more and more of the production of bromine and magnesium in the United States has shifted from sea water to natural brines and evaporites found in continental rocks. At present, virtually no bromine is produced from sea water in this country. It is obvious, however, that for countries without large brine and evaporite deposits, such as Japan and the Scandinavian countries, the prospect of a marine supply for bromine and magnesium remains attractive.

Table 6–6

Salts Laid Down During Concentration of Sea Water (grams)*

Volume (liters)	Fe_2O_3	$CaCO_3$	$CaSO_4$ $\cdot 2H_2O$	NaCl	$MgSO_4$	$MgCl_2$	NaBr	KCl
1.000	–	–	–	–	–	–	–	–
0.533	0.0030	0.0642	–	–	–	–	–	–
0.316	–	trace	–	–	–	–	–	–
0.245	–	trace	–	–	–	–	–	–
0.190	–	0.0530	0.5600	–	–	–	–	–
0.1445	–	–	0.5620	–	–	–	–	–
0.131	–	–	0.1840	–	–	–	–	–
0.112	–	–	0.1600	–	–	–	–	–
0.095	–	–	0.0508	3.2614	0.0040	0.0078	–	–
0.064	–	–	0.1476	9.6500	0.0130	0.0356	–	–
0.039	–	–	0.0700	7.8960	0.0262	0.0434	0.0728	–
0.0302	–	–	0.0144	2.6240	0.0174	0.0150	0.0358	–
0.023	–	–	–	2.2720	0.0254	0.0240	0.0518	–
0.0162	–	–	–	1.4040	0.5382	0.0274	0.0620	–
0.0000	–	–	–	2.5885	1.8545	3.1640	0.3300	0.5339
Total:	0.0030	0.1172	1.7488	29.6959	2.4787	3.3172	0.5524	0.5339

*After Usiglio, 1849.

With these conditions in mind, we will discuss the present-day technology and economics of the three major chemicals extracted from sea water: sodium chloride, magnesium, and bromine.

Sodium Chloride

From the oldest times the sea has been a source of salt for human consumption. In order to obtain "common salt" from sea water, we use the energy of the Sun to evaporate the water, leaving behind the residual salt. This salt (sometimes called "solar salt" because of the method of concentration) is not necessarily pure sodium chloride. Indeed, as can be seen in Table 6–6, different compounds will deposit as evaporation proceeds. In order to obtain pure sodium chloride, a sequence of evaporating basins is required, such as those at the Leslie Salt Company plant in San Francisco Bay (Fig. 6–2). In the first evaporating pond, evaporation proceeds until the salt concentration increases from the normal sea water concentration of about 3 percent to about 26 percent. From Table 6–6 we see that calcium carbonate in small quantities and calcium sulfate will precipitate out. The remaining brine is then transferred to another evaporating pond

FIGURE 6-2 *Salt produced by solar evaporation of sea water in San Francisco Bay. Courtesy of the Leslie Salt Co.*

and evaporation continues. Almost pure sodium chloride precipitates there. When 90 percent of the available sodium chloride has been precipitated, the residual liquids, called bitterns, are drained off. The bitterns are enriched in potassium and magnesium and would be a source of these metals if evaporite and continental brine deposits were not cheaper to work.

The resulting sodium chloride is commonly as much as 99.6 percent pure when dry. Much of the solar salt produced in other countries has not been as pure as that produced in San Francisco Bay. However, new ventures in the Bahamas by the Diamond Crystal Salt Company, in Baja California, Mexico, by National Bulk Carrier, and in Bonaire, Netherlands, West Indies, by International Salt Company will result in the availability of large quantities of high-quality sodium chloride for further processing.

The major use of sodium chloride, aside from direct human consumption and use as a de-icer on highways, is in the manufacture of sodium hydroxide, commonly called caustic soda or lye, sodium metal, hydrochloric acid, and chlorine gas. Because all these processes involve the breaking of strong chemical bonds, they require a large amount of energy. For this reason, the accessibility of the sodium chloride source, whether mined or derived from sea water, to a large amount of cheap electrical energy is one of the important conditions for economic exploitation of a sodium chloride source. The other condition is that the resulting product be used fairly close to its production site in order to keep transportation costs to a minimum.

Solar salt produced in the Bahamas, for example, will be inexpensively transported northward by ship or barge, using the flow of the Gulf Stream, and will be processed in the northeastern United States. The processed sodium and chlorine compounds (or the elemental forms) will be used in the Northeast factories for the production of plastics and in other manufacturing processes.

Magnesium

The demand for magnesium is not very large at the present time. Indeed, all the major powers appear to have more magnesium stockpiled than they can find uses for.

Although sea water was an important source for magnesium in the past, this element is now being obtained more and more from brine wells and, in the United States in particular, from the Great Salt Lake in Utah. It can also be obtained from the sedimentary rock containing dolomite—$CaMg(CO_3)_2$. This is a fairly common rock type, and processes for the extraction of magnesium have now been worked out. (Indeed, calcined dolomite can be used in the place of calcined calcium carbonate in the process for the extraction of magnesium from sea water discussed below. This replacement would increase the yield of magnesium in the process.) The cost at the moment is slightly more than the cost of extraction from concentrated magnesium-rich brines, but in the future, should the need for magnesium increase compared to its availability from its normal sources, dolomite could be a competitor with the extraction from sea water. The most important consideration here becomes the cost of power to extract the magnesium from the various alternatives to concentrated brines. A concentrated brine or sea water source that does not have cheap power close by will yield more expensive magnesium than a dolomite source close to cheap power.

The procedure for magnesium recovery from sea water takes advantage of the fact that if sea water is made more and more basic, magnesium hydroxide will precipitate out. This precipitate can then be collected and processed further to obtain magnesium metal or purified magnesium salt. The detailed process (Fig. 6–3) is as follows: Sea water is continuously fed through tanks to which an excess of milk of lime (a water slurry of calcium oxide) is added in excess. The amount is sufficient both to precipitate the magnesium hydroxide and to retain the undesirable element boron in solution. The sea water, once stripped of magnesium, is discarded.

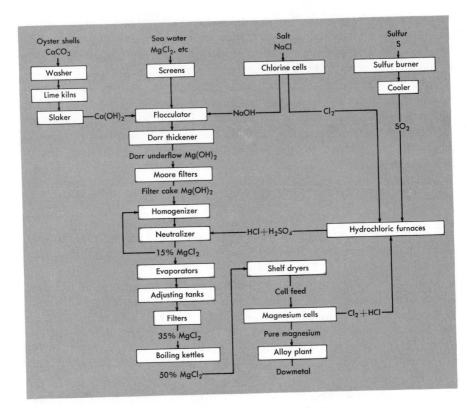

FIGURE 6-3 *Flow diagram for the production of manganese from sea water. Courtesy of the Dow Chemical Company.*

The magnesium hydroxide precipitate, together with some impurities, settles in a settling tank, then is converted to magnesium chloride by the addition of hydrochloric acid, and evaporated to a concentrated solution (about 35 percent magnesium chloride by weight). Calcium, which has entered the system during processing and is not wanted, is precipitated and removed by the controlled addition of magnesium sulfate. The resulting precipitate of calcium sulfate, plus any sodium chloride present, is allowed to settle out and is discarded. The purified magnesium chloride solution is further concentrated, then heated to 170°C to convert it into a solid hydrated magnesium chloride salt suitable for the electrolytic production of magnesium metal.

The electrolytic cells are maintained at 700°C to support a fused salt mixture (25% $MgCl_2$, 15% $CaCl_2$, 60% NaCl) in a steel tub that acts as the cathode. Suspended graphite electrodes are anodes. The solid hydrated magnesium chloride cell feed is added continuously to maintain the proper composition as magnesium and chlorine are generated at the electrodes. The molten magnesium floats on the fused salt mixture and is ladeled off, and the chlorine gas is piped away, after cooling, to a hydrochloric acid-generating plant.

It is obvious from this description of the process that, besides sea water, four other ingredients must be available cheaply in order to make the process economical: (a) a source of pure calcium carbonate (or pure dolomite as a possible alternate) that, by kilning, will supply calcium oxide, (b) a source of hydrochloric acid—ultimately made, as we have seen, from sodium chloride, (c) a source of sulfur to make magnesium sulfate, and (d) a source of cheap electrical power.

The Dow Chemical Company plant in Freeport, Texas, seemed ideally suited for magnesium extraction from sea water because all these items were available locally at relatively low cost. Oyster shells dredged from Galveston Bay provide the relatively pure calcium carbonate; Gulf Coast salt domes provide cheap local sources of both sodium chloride and sulfur, while oil, suitable for power generation has, of course, been the raw material for which Texas has become most famous.

Magnesium metal is lighter than aluminum and has been used, after proper alloying to provide better working properties, where lightness and strength are required. There are other uses as well, but magnesium does not yet command the importance and utility of its close cousin, aluminum.

In terms of quantity, the major use of magnesium is as magnesia (MgO) and other magnesium compounds. These items are used in pharmaceuticals and in chemical processing.

Bromine

Until quite recently much of the bromine production in the United States also came from sea water. Now, however, most of it is from concentrated subsurface brines that provide a high-grade raw material close to power sources. Nevertheless, it is instructive to follow the sea water extraction process, for it is potentially useful in other parts of the world.

The main use of bromine has been in the production of ethylene dibromide, used with tetraethyl lead, as an antiknock agent in gasoline. Its role is to volatilize the lead as lead bromide and to prevent its accumulation in the automobile engine. Recent retrenchment in the use of tetraethyl lead has adversely affected the use of bromine as well. Another use of bromine is in the manufacture of compounds suitable for fire-proofing wooden structures. This usage is still in the exploratory stages, however, with major questions regarding possible local bromine release to the atmosphere in the case of a large fire.

Figure 6–4 shows the process used to manufacture liquid bromine from

The chemical resources of sea water

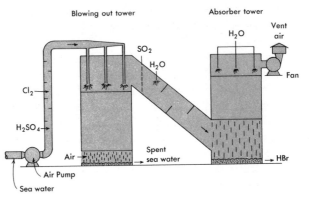

FIGURE 6-4 *Diagrammatic representation of bromine production from the sea. Sea water is pumped into a vertical mixing chamber into which acid and chlorine are added in the proportions required to convert the dissolved bromide into elemental bromine. The treated sea water is distributed over the top of a tower similar to a cooling tower. As it passes downward, a stream of air passing up sweeps the volatile bromine out of the water. Courtesy of the Dow Chemical Company.*

sea water by the Dow Chemical Company. Filtered, preheated sea water is pumped into a chamber into which chlorine gas and sulfuric acid are introduced, thereby releasing bromine as a gas. The gaseous bromine is stripped from sea water by a stream of air acting through a spray of the sea water containing the elemental bromine. The bromine is then converted to hydrobromic acid by the action of sulfur dioxide on a water vapor-bromine gas mixture. The condensed hydrobromic acid-sulfuric acid solution is then transferred and treated with chlorine gas again to release a pure bromine gas that, on condensation, becomes liquid bromine. The bromine, in turn, is reacted with ethylene to produce ethylene dibromide, the principal form in which bromine is marketed.

Desalination

There is one chemical compound, water, that we obtain perpetually from the oceans. As we have seen in Chapter 2, the transport of water from the oceans to the land through atmospheric precipitation proceeds at a fairly rapid rate. The mean residence time of a water molecule in the oceans, before it goes through its journey to the continents and back to the sea as a stream, is about 4×10^4 years. The Sun does the work of releasing the water molecules as vapor from salty sea water; and the global atmospheric circulation system, also driven by the energy of the Sun, brings this fresh water to the land as rain.

The controlled harnessing of the Sun's energy for the purpose of evaporation of water is being done in arid areas close to the sea, using glass shelters, similar to greenhouses. Evaporation of sea water occurs under the hot Sun during the day, and condensation then occurs at night on the chilled glass roof surfaces. By this process, a humid, almost tropical environment is maintained on a small scale as a man-made oasis in the coastal desert.

Such a project has been developed in North America with

Table 7-1

Representative Salinities of Some Waters

Type of Water	Salinity or Total Dissolved Solids (parts per million)
Sea water	35,000
Average streams	120
Some nonpotable ground waters	3,000
Potable "hard" or salty waters	500
Certain Maine lakes	10

the financial assistance of some of the "oil sheikdoms" of the Arabian Peninsula, with the prospect of developing a small local specialty agriculture within those countries. Although the program is interesting for its potential in changing the life style of a small population, it is not aimed at solving the water problem of large populations. To do so we must use other methods and man-made energy.

The purpose of desalination is to replicate nature's process at a particular location, using man-made energy transfer devices. It is the process of extracting low salinity water (maximally 300 to 500 ppm dissolved solids) suitable for drinking, industry, or agriculture from water so saline as to be unsuitable for these purposes. Sea water is the most obvious raw material for desalination, but the processes are also applicable to salty waters in aquifers on land or those resulting from industrial and municipal salting during use or after treatment for purification. Some representative waters with their amounts of total dissolved solids are given in Table 7-1.

Methods of Desalination

The simplest desalination device is the old-fashioned still. The sea water is heated to boiling, and the salt-free vapor is condensed by a circulating cold-water jacket around the tube attached to the heating chamber (Fig. 7-1). Although this technique is used in some small-scale operations to obtain urgently required drinking water, it loses so much heat to the circulating coolant water that it is far too inefficient to provide the large-scale needs of communities at a reasonable cost.

In order to reduce power consumption, several methods of desalination are presently being tried either in working plants or in pilot plants. They are 1. multistage flash distillation; 2. long-tube vertical evaporation; 3. elec-

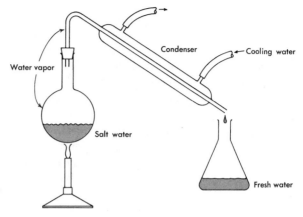

FIGURE 7-1 *The principle of the simple still.*

trodialysis; 4. reverse osmosis; 5. freezing; 6. crystallization. The first two methods are improvements on the old-fashioned still; the others involve the harnessing of quite different but well-known physical processes. We will consider each of the methods briefly.

Multistage Flash Distillation

Figure 7–2 is a diagrammatic representation of a multistage flash distillation system similar to one used at Elat, Israel, on the Gulf of Aqaba, where the temperature of the surface sea water entering the system is unusually high. As the sea water enters the system and travels along in a pipe exposed to a set of successive chambers, it is progressively heated as a result of the release of heat due to condensation of fresh water vapor along the relatively cooler intake pipe. If the intake sea water starts at 29°C (sea water heated by the 36°C outflow water), by the end of the final stage it

FIGURE 7-2 *Multistage flash distillation system.*

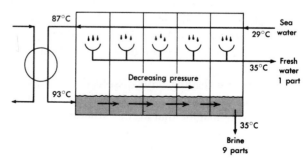

Multi-stage distilation (Elat model) That is why temperatures are high.

is at 87°C, because the sea water in this last chamber on the outflow side has been heated through a heat exchanger to 93°C. Thus the outflowing sea water, as it becomes more and more salty on its way to the discharge port, is also cooling off. At each stage, however, it is warmer than the water entering through the intake pipe.

The "flashing" takes place because at each stage the heated water is introduced into a chamber under vacuum. As the temperature of the brine decreases, the pressure in each subsequent chamber is also decreased in order to continue the flash evaporation as the heated water hits the chamber. Vapor formed by flashing heats the intake pipes as it releases heat during condensation on a suitable surface; the condensate is then tapped as desalinated water.

Long-tube Vertical Evaporation

An alternative multistage technique involves the use of long tubes along which heat exchange and resulting condensation take place (Fig. 7–3). In any particular stage, sea water at a temperature higher than the previous stage but lower than the next, because of the heat-exchange process, is allowed to fall as a thin film along the inner walls of a tube, the outer parts of which are exposed to warmer vapor from a higher temperature stage closer to the source of heating. The hot vapor condenses by heat transfer to the cooler sea water. The condensate is trapped, and the warmer sea water and associated vapor are transferred away from the stage—the vapor to the next cooler stage (toward the intake) and the water toward the source of heat.

Many new desalination plants take advantage of a complex system of multistage flash distillation and long-tube vertical evaporation.

Electrodialysis

When electrodes attached to a battery are immersed in a saline solution, current flows through the wires because the circuit is closed by the flow of charged particles—ions—in the saline solution. The positively charged ions are attracted to the negatively charged electrode (on the electron-rich side of the battery), which is called the cathode, and the negatively charged ions move toward the electron deficient electrode (positively charged), called the anode.

If we are dealing with dissolved sodium chloride, the sodium ion (Na^+) will go to the cathode and the chloride ion (Cl^-) will go to the anode.

We can imagine that at the cathode

$$Na^+ + electron = Na^\circ(metal)$$

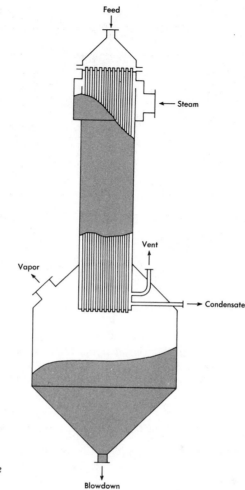

FIGURE 7-3 *Long-tube vertical evaporator.*

but metallic sodium would immediately react with water to release hydrogen:

$$2Na^\circ + 2H_2O = 2Na^+ + 2OH^- + H_2$$

and hydrogen would bubble up from the cathode.

The net reaction is therefore written

$$2Na^+ + 2 \text{ electron} + 2H_2O = 2Na^+ + 2OH^- + H_2$$

At the anode, an electron must be transported from the solution because it cannot become charged. The reaction at the anode then becomes

$$2Cl^- = Cl_2 + 2 \text{ electrons}$$

Hence chlorine gas will bubble off from the anode.

Desalination

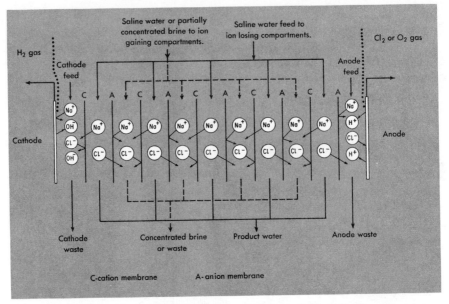

FIGURE 7-4 *The principle of electrodialytic method of desalination.*

FIGURE 7-5 *The cost of electrodialytic desalination as a function of salinity of feed water. After E. R. Gilliland, 1965,* First International Smposium on Water Desalination, *October 3–9, Washington, SWD/90.*

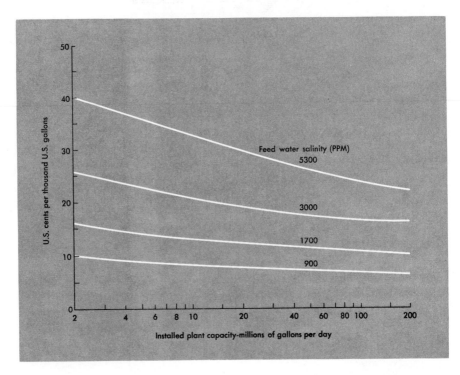

This basic principle is used in electrodialysis. The fundamental change in converting a simple electrolytic cell into an electrodialysis cell is shown in Fig. 7–4. The original electrolytic cell is partitioned by ion-exchange membranes that pass either cations such as sodium or anions such as chloride. Proceeding from the cathode, these are placed alternately, first a cation-passing membrane, then an anion-passing membrane, and so forth until the anode is reached. The last membrane before the anode is an anion-passing membrane.

The water from one chamber cannot pass to another chamber; only the ions can. Starting with saline water in all the chambers, we apply a current. All the cations will immediately move toward the cathode and all the anions will move toward the anode. Because each type of ion is passed only by its specific type of membrane, the net effect is to concentrate the salt in alternate chambers, leaving the ones in between depleted in salt. The fresh water is tapped for use, and the concentrated brine is discarded.

Electrodialysis is most useful for slightly saline waters. The costs go up sharply with increasing salinity (Fig. 7–5). It has been used to make potable water from alkaline well waters in the midwestern United States by reducing the salt concentration from about 3000 ppm to less than 500 ppm. It is also used in eliminating excess salts from some industrial and treated municipal waters.

Reverse Osmosis

If we take an open tube partially filled with salt water, enclose one end with a thin sheet of cellophane, and lower the enclosed end into a beaker of distilled water, we note a rise in the water level inside the tube, indicating the transport of water across the cellophane boundary from the distilled water to the salt-water solution (Fig. 7–6). We also note that there is no transport of salt back through the cellophane into the beaker. The cellophane is therefore acting as a semipermeable membrane permitting

FIGURE 7-6   *The principle of the reverse osmosis method of desalination.*

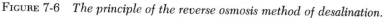
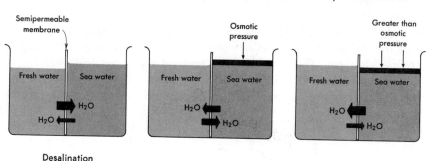

Desalination

the transport of water but not the dissolved ions. The process is called *osmosis*.

Now if we put a piston in the tube containing the salt water and apply just enough pressure to prevent the water level from rising, we will have a measure of the size of the force drawing the fresh water from the beaker to the tube. This is called the *osmotic pressure*.

We deduce from this experiment that if we can stop the flow of water from the fresh water reservoir to the salty-water reservoir by applying sufficient pressure on the latter, then we should be able to "push" water across the cellophane membrane from the salt-water tube to the fresh water in the beaker. This transport of water from a salty solution across a semipermeable membrane by the application of pressure is called *reverse osmosis*.

Like electrodialysis, its primary use will probably be in the desalting of saline continental or sewage effluent waters rather than in the desalting of sea water although, in principle, it can be applied to any salt solution. Its advantage is that the process does not have to be run continuously to be economic. It is possible to use power at low-use times when it is cheaper to provide the pressure by pumping. Thus it would not require a separate, continuously operating power plant as do the distillation methods.

Freezing

When sea water is cooled sufficiently, ice forms at the surface. Thus the entire Arctic Ocean is covered by "sea ice." Salt is excluded from the crystal lattice of ice, but it is commonly included to some degree in "sea ice" as tiny grains between the ice crystals. This process, observed in nature, can be used to extract fresh water from sea water.

The process actually involves using a coolant—that is, a material added to the sea water that vaporizes easily and in so doing extracts its heat of vaporization from the surface of the water from which it is evaporating. If enough heat is extracted, the water will freeze. The ice so formed has less of the entrapped salt grains than natural sea ice and, on melting, is suitable for man's personal and industrial uses.

The refrigerant commonly used is *n*-butane (boiling point: $-0.5°C$). The butane, already at several degrees centigrade below the freezing temperature of water, is bubbled through sea water. As the butane evaporates, it cools the surface of the water below the temperature of initial freezing and ice crystals form. The crystals grow upward along vertical columns that are washed free of salt grains by a counterflow of a part of the fresh water that results from the melting of the ice. The melting of the ice is accelerated by the condensation of the butane in an adjacent tub. The brine that is to be rejected is twice as salty as the original sea water, and the butane is reused in the process after cooling. The product water contains less than 0.1 ppm butane and 100 ppm dissolved salts and is potable.

The estimated expense for a freeze-desalting plant under construction in Ipswich, England, is about 48 cents per 1000 gallons. Although more expensive than unprocessed water, it is considerably cheaper than water obtained by distillation. The low temperature of the North Sea waters aids the freezing operation and reduces costs.

Crystallization

It is possible to use another hydrocarbon, propane, in the desalting of water. In this case, however, advantage is taken of the fact that propane forms a hydrate with water at low temperatures. As propane is introduced into cool sea water, it evaporates and extracts heat from the sea water reservoir. Both the propane and the water are cooled, thus resulting in the formation of crystals having about 17 molecules of water to 1 molecule of propane. These crystals are isolated and melted by the heat given off by the condensation of the propane vapor. On melting, the crystals form two liquid layers that are immiscible, one of pure propane and the other of pure, virtually salt-free water.

This method is not being developed at present on a large scale but may someday provide an alternative procedure to the freezing method in temperate regions where surface sea water is already relatively cool.

The Economics of Desalination

The fact that desalination of sea water is technically feasible does not automatically make it the solution to all the world's water problems. There are two fundamental considerations in addition to the technical feasibility of any specific desalination method: (a) the cost of the water obtained, especially in relation to alternative, possibly unconventional sources, and (b) the effects on coastal ecology of the dumping of the hot concentrated brine residue from the water-extraction process.

The human use of water is of two types: potable water for domestic and industrial uses, and water for agricultural purposes. Compared to agricultural needs, the per capita potable-water requirements are low; and the cost of supplying to areas without adequate natural water supplies can be offset by various intrinsic values of the area based on climate, cultural, strategic, or other considerations. Similarly, the cost of water is normally a small part of the ultimate cost of many industrial products and can be absorbed even in a competitive market. On the other hand, the cost of water for irrigation is often a significant part of the total cost of agricultural products. The cost of all desalinated water is still considerably higher than the reasonable cost that can be added to staple crops without destroying their competitive stance relative to more cheaply produced crops using natural supplies of fresh water where this occurs. The only way out of this dilemma appears to be in the development of large (population = 100,000 or more) communities which can use the power of a nuclear reactor for desalination for agricultural purposes and for the industrial processing of raw materials. Such nuclear complexes (or "nuplexes") might then be economically viable.

In certain semiarid regions, such as Italy and southeastern France, nearby through-flowing rivers or mountain streams provide water, via aqueducts, for agricultural purposes as well as for drinking. The major arid parts of the world are not so fortunate, however. Figure 7–7 is a map showing the mean annual precipitation around the Earth. Arid regions are found as two globe-encircling strips approximately between 20° to 30° north and 20° to 30° south, except on the eastern side of the continents. In addition, areas of low precipitation occur on the leeward side of major mountain systems, such as in Nevada and Utah. (The prevailing world-encircling winds at these latitudes are from west to east—the Sierra Nevada of California acting as a trap for the atmospheric moisture derived from the Pacific Ocean.)

Obviously, from what has been said, desalination as a source of water for drinking or industrial purposes will depend on the competitiveness of water obtained by desalination versus that obtained by other means. A series of examples and alternatives to desalination will best illustrate the options that must be considered when planning for the water economy of a populated region.

A large number of desalination plants have been put into operation in the islands of the Caribbean. Most of the smaller islands can only support the sought-after tourist population by increasing and regulating water supplies. Normal water-catching procedures, so picturesquely represented by the stepped rooftops of many Bermuda cottages, are not sufficient for a densely clustered additional population. In this case, the cost of desalination is compensated for by the increased value of land because of the increased tourist influx.

In addition to the tourist uses, desalination in the Caribbean has been forced on the U.S. Navy Base at Guantanamo, Cuba, for strategic reasons. Most of the larger islands of the Caribbean generally have enough high land to provide moisture traps for the water-ladened tropical air, and the resulting streams provide a suitable supply of water.

If care is not taken to locate the desalination plant where easy exchange with the open sea exists, it is possible that hot waste brines may accumulate in basins on the island shelves. Most of the Caribbean does not support a particularly high marine productivity; thus such an additional stress may

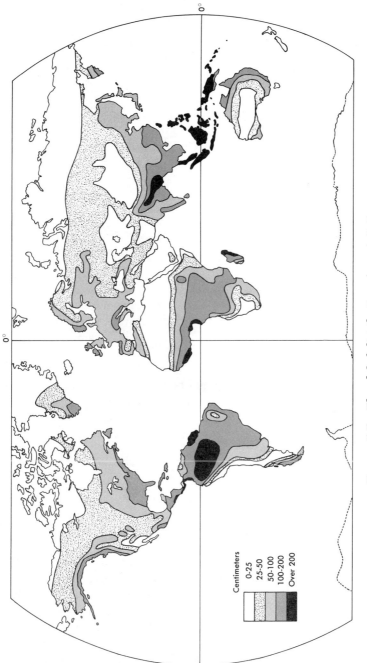

Centimeters

0-25

25-50

50-100

100-200

Over 200

FIGURE 7-7 *The global distribution of precipitation.*

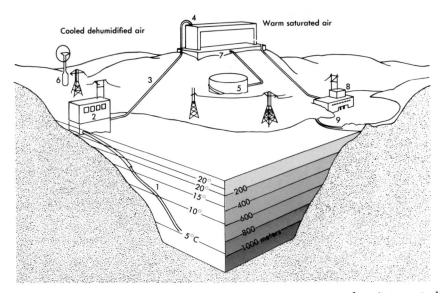

FIGURE 7-8 *Schematic representation of a water recovery plan for tropical regions by condensation using deep water as coolant. After R. D. Gerard and O. A. Roels, 1970, Mar. Tech. Soc. Jour., v. 4, pp. 96–79.*

be detrimental to the useful marine fisheries that may exist. For this reason, a novel approach to the production of fresh water is being explored—namely, the extraction of air moisture from tropical air, utilizing the cooling action of cold (approximately 5°C), deep water pumped to the surface (Fig. 7-8).

A model calculation for such an operation is shown in Table 7-2. When one considers that in the trade-wind belt 200 million gallons of fresh water passes as vapor in the air across an island with a 2-mile circumference every day and that half of this amount is potentially extractable, one can understand the reasons for exploring this process as an alternative to desalination. In addition to the water, however, certain other advantages are possible with this system. Note that the exit air temperature is 12°C; therefore what is essentially a method for air conditioning is available. Also, the deep waters of the oceans are richer in nutrient elements, such as nitrogen and phosphorus, than surface waters. Thus there is the prospect of increased productivity from these waters if they are localized in bays for the production of shellfish through mariculture.

Another alternative to desalination is the use of the ice stored around the two major ice caps of the world, Greenland and Antarctica. Although suggestions for the use of icebergs, or even sea ice, from the Arctic Ocean have been offered, the first quantitative economic assessment showing the competitiveness of this source was made for the Antarctic source. As the Antarctic ice cap encounters the ocean in shelf areas, it continues seaward until it floats as the water deepens. Thus large, flat slabs of shelf ice are formed. These slabs are relatively free of sea-salt inclusions because the

Table 7–2

Conditions for the Extraction of Atmospheric Water
in the Trade-Wind Belt
by Deep-Water Cooled Condensation*

	In	Out
Deep-water temperature (from meters after pumping)	5.5°C	10°C
Air temperature	25°C	12°C
Humidity	75%	100%
Water content of air (percent by weight)	1.5%	0.88%

This means one liter of water requires 161 kg of air processed and 245 kg of sea water processed.

*After O. A. Roels.

major part of the slabs was produced on land from snow rather than by freezing of sea water.

The icebergs from the Ross shelf in Antarctica (Fig. 7–9) could be supplied to the arid lands of western South America; the Amery shelf could supply icebergs for haulage to western Australia, which is also very arid; and the Filchner ice shelf could be the site of supply of icebergs for use along the west African coast.

The cost calculation assumes that an iceberg from one of these shelf sites could be hauled by a tug to the site of its use for about $1 million. The cost per gallon for transport would depend on the size of the iceberg that is successfully hauled by the tug. If a tug can pull an iceberg 250 yards thick and 2700 yards on each edge from the Amery shelf to the northwest coast of Australia, 207 billion gallons of water would be available, provided that precautions were taken to catch the melting iceberg in a suitable plastic catchment basin so as to prevent loss to the sea. If the cost can be kept this low, it is considerably less than the cost of desalination. Indeed, the cost is within the allowable range for the economic use of the water for agricultural purposes.

The very long distance transport of water to arid regions by pipelines is another alternative to desalination that must be considered. For example, the need for water in Southern California and Arizona could be met by tapping the Columbia River in the Pacific Northwest. The estimated cost for a long-term operation, including interest on the borrowed money and maintenance, has been estimated as between 22 and 37 cents per 1000 gal-

FIGURE 7-9 *Three Navy ships move a huge iceberg in McMurdo Sound, Antarctica. Such an iceberg might be suitable for transport to regions deficient in fresh water. Courtesy of U.S. Navy.*

lons. The cheapest desalinated water at present costs 75 cents per 1000 gallons.

The effects of intercepting large volumes of water, however, and of transporting them great distances must be considered. For the West Coast of the United States, one effect would be to diminish the discharge of the Columbia River into the sea and thereby to influence the properties at the mouth of the river where the delicate balance of fresh and sea water occurs.

The Aswan Dam in Egypt has increased the amount of sea water intrusion into the fertile delta of the Nile, and the interruption of silt supply to the delta by the dam has already resulted in coastal erosion eastward of the delta by waves and longshore transport.

Similarly, it has recently been argued that if fresh water from the Sacramento River were extensively deflected for municipal, industrial, or agricultural uses, an undesirable effect could well be an increased pollution of the South Bay of San Francisco, which has no fresh water flowing into it at all. The reason is that the flushing of South Bay depends on the supply of excess fresh water from the northern arm of San Francisco Bay, into which the Sacramento River debouches. (Fig. 2–10).

Consequently, deflection or damming of fresh water sources, although attractive as an option to the more-expensive and possibly salt-polluting desalination process, must be considered with regional and long-range planning clearly in mind. It is for this reason that the Ipswich desalination enterprise, using the freezing method, has been commissioned. Ipswich, in the east coast county of Suffolk, in England, needs to augment its present water supply by about 1 million gallons a day. Because of the quality of rivers and the value of land uses in areas where reservoirs might be possible, it was considered more reasonable to use desalination rather than natural fresh water from remote regions. The east coast of England receives less rain than the west coast, has fewer hilly terrains, and has no large rivers flowing through it. The plant is to be in operation in 1973.

8

Pollution of the oceans

The transport of materials from the continents to the oceans is a massive and unrelenting process. Rivers and winds transport substances in both solid and soluble forms, injecting them into coastal waters and the open sea. We can ✻ consider any man-induced modification of this natural process as "pollution" if it sensibly alters the quality of the environment or interferes with some broadly beneficial use of an area. The modifications may take either of two general forms. Pollution may be the result of the addition of man-made materials, particularly chemicals alien to the natural world, or it may be an increase above the normal level of concentration of naturally occurring materials. ✻

Pollution of the Coastal Zone and Open Ocean

The coastal zone of the ocean is the region most heavily hit by man-induced changes. Because of the intense activity there, it is also the region of the most massive public concern in the field of marine pollution. The open ocean, however, may also become polluted by wind transport of materials from continents, by ocean surface circulation or bottom transport from polluted coastal zones, or by the deliberate or accidental dumping of materials from ships.

Pollution of estuarine waters is spreading rapidly because of the ever-growing population and intensification of industrial activity along the coasts relative to the interiors of continents. There are many reasons for the growing population density along coastal areas, but one of the most important, as well as most disturbing, is that more and more industries are making the trek toward the coast in part because they need larger depositories for the waste they produce. Industrial expansion in continental interiors is limited, for rivers and ground waters of highly industrialized countries are rapidly being taxed to the capacity permissible by a population requiring high standards of environmental purity. The only seemingly infinite site as a dumping ground is the oceans.

As we shall see, this attitude has already placed a heavy burden on the coastline; and before any additional and possibly irreversible damages result, we must focus our scientific and managerial efforts on the problem.

A major avenue of potential pollution in the open oceans is through atmospheric transport. The potential atmospheric flux of man-mobilized materials is quite large, as can be seen in Table 8–1. Much of this material is washed out in the coastal zones by rainfall, but what remains is transported by means of the tropospheric wind systems (moving from west to east in the highly populated temperate zone).

When air-transported materials reach the ocean surface, they will be moved around the major ocean-surface gyre systems (Fig. 2–15). The rate of surface-water circulation is quite rapid, and it takes only 5 to 10 years for a complete hemispheric circuit for each major ocean basin.

Another major method of injecting pollutants into the open ocean is by means of shipping. Ships are primarily responsible for the dumping of oil, either accidentally or by the programmed flushing of oil tankers after discharging the oil at the terminal. Today, the flotsam and jetsam also commonly associated with shipping have been supplemented by the arrival on the scene, since World War II, of widely dispersed fine-grained plastics. These small (0.25 to 0.5 cm) particles have been observed in the Sargasso Sea of the North Atlantic at concentrations of about 4000 per square kilometer of ocean surface. The significance of these particles as a pollutant or as an indicator of pollution is still to be assessed.

Table 8–1

Amounts of Elements Mobilized into the Atmosphere as a Result of the Combustion of Fossil Fuels*

Element	Fossil Fuel Mobilization ($\times 10^9$ grams/year)		
	Coal	Oil	Total
Li	9		
Be	0.41	0.00006	0.41
B	10.5	0.0003	10.5
Na	280	0.33	280
Mg	280	0.02	280
Al	1400	0.08	1400
P	70		
S	2800	550	3400
Cl	140		
K	140		
Ca	1400	0.82	1400
Sc	0.7	0.0002	0.7
Ti	70	0.02	70
V	3.5	8.2	12
Cr	1.4	0.05	1.5
Mn	7	0.02	7
Fe	1400	0.41	1400
Co	0.7	0.03	0.7
Ni	2.1	1.6	3.7
Cu	2.1	0.023	2.1
Zn	7	0.04	7
Ga	1	0.002	1
Ge	0.7	0.0002	0.7
As	0.7	0.002	0.7
Se	0.42	0.03	0.45
Rb	14		
Sr	70	0.02	70
Y	1.4	0.0002	1.4
Mo	0.7	1.6	2.3
Ag	0.07	0.00002	0.07
Cd		0.002	
Sn	0.28	0.002	0.28
Ba	70	0.02	70
La	1.4	0.0008	1.4
Ce	1.6	0.002	1.6
Pr	0.31		
Nd	0.65		
Sm	0.22		

*After K. K. Bertine and E. D. Goldberg, 1971, *Science*, v. 173, pp. 233–235.

Table 8-1 (cont.)

Element	Fossil Fuel Mobilization ($\times$ 10⁹ grams/year)		
	Coal	Oil	Total
Eu	0.1		
Gd	0.22		
Tb	0.042		
Ho	0.042		
Er	0.085	0.0002	0.085
Tm	0.014		
Yb	0.07		
Lu	0.01		
Re	0.007		
Hg	0.0017	1.6	1.6
Pb	3.5	0.05	3.6
Bi	0.75		
U	0.14	0.001	0.14

The Major Pollutants in the Sea

The potentially polluting materials dumped or injected into the ocean are divisible into five major types: 1. bulk material, such as sewage sludge and dredge spoils; 2. phosphates and other materials that affect the biological cycles of the sea; 3. the so-called heavy metals, such as mercury; 4. petroleum and its products; and 5. chlorinated hydrocarbons, such as the pesticide DDT and the industrial chemicals termed PCB (polychlorinated biphenyls).

Bulk Material Dumping

The bulk materials dumped into the ocean are of several types: 1. Those associated with consumer uses; 2. Those associated with industrial plants; 3. Those associated with construction; and 4. Those related to military and other strategic activities.

The total yearly mass of bulk material dumped into the oceans from all these sources in the offshore waters of the United States has been assessed in a report by the Council on Environmental Quality. The results are shown in Table 8-2. The materials associated with municipal sewage and consumer product use are listed as "sewage sludge" and "solid waste," respectively. Disposal of refuse and garbage in the ocean is a feature only of the Pacific Coast at the present, although it was dumped off New York City until the early 1930s. In most other places it is put in sanitary land fills or processed by incinerators.

Table 8-2

Types and Amounts of Material
Dumped into the Oceans by the United States* (in tons)

Waste Type	Atlantic	Gulf	Pacific	Total	Percent of Total
Dredge spoils	15,808,000	15,300,000	7,320,000	38,428,000	80
Industrial wastes	3,013,200	696,000	981,300	4,690,500	10
Sewage sludge	4,477,000	0	0	4,477,000	9
Construction and demolition debris	574,000	0	0	574,000	<1
Solid waste	0	0	26,000	26,000	<1
Explosives	15,200	0	0	15,200	<1
Total	23,887,400	15,966,000	8,327,300	48,210,700	100

*After *Ocean Dumping*, 1970, Council on Environmental Quality.

Industrial wastes include the chemical off-scouring of the massive petrochemical and paper industries, although the basic metals industries contribute the major burden (Table 8–3). Many of the materials released are toxic organic compounds, acids, and heavy metals potentially capable of polluting if improperly located. They are generally placed in containers before being dumped in the sea. However, the method of dumping may involve puncturing the containers at sea to permit its sinking. The escaping chemicals could be detrimental to marine life.

Construction wastes come from two sources. Dredging operations, mainly

Table 8-3

Industrial Wastes Dumped into the Ocean*

Type of Waste	Estimated Tonnage	Percent
Waste acids	2,720,500	58
Refinery wastes	562,900	12
Pesticide wastes	328,300	7
Paper mill wastes	140,700	3
Other wastes	938,100	20

*After *Ocean Dumping*, 1970, Council on Environmental Quality.

for navigation and harbor maintenance, are by far the largest man-activated contributors of materials to the ocean. Much of the dredged material (called "dredge spoils") is taken from harbor areas that are commonly heavily polluted by sewage sludge and industrial wastes. It has been estimated, for example, that 45 percent of the dredge spoils in the Atlantic is polluted in one way or another. For the Gulf Coast and the Pacific Coast, the figures are 31 and 19 percent, respectively.

Another large contribution to construction wastes comes from debris from demolition and building activities. The debris from construction in New York City, for example, amounts to about 500,000 tons dumped into the oceans annually. Most other coastal cities have adequate landfill areas to accommodate the construction debris. Large areas of many coastal cities are built on filled land made from deposits of these wastes. (Fig. 1–2).

Although explosives, chemical munitions, and radioactive wastes have all been dumped into the sea at some time in the past, the more recent policy of most countries is to limit dumping of strategic materials only to explosives. Radioactive wastes are normally placed in large storage depots on land. Chemical munitions are increasingly treated to eliminate their toxic effects.

The sites of ocean dumping, past and present, for different types of materials are shown in Fig. 8–1 for the United States. The amount of ocean dumping has been increasing each year (Fig. 8–2).

Phosphate and Eutrophication

Aqueous life depends on the availability of dissolved nitrogen and phosphorus. Regions of high nitrogen and phosphorus concentrations in the ocean, for example, are sites of high biological productivity. If phosphorus and nitrogen are added to water bodies by the action of man, there is the possibility of excessive growth of the minute unicellular plants (called *phytoplankton*) that mark the beginning of the food chain in the aqueous medium. This process has been called *eutrophication* and was first noted for lakes, where it is commonly observed.

As the organic particles resulting from high surface productivity fall through the water column, they are metabolized by using the dissolved oxygen of the body of water. When all the oxygen is used up, the deeper water becomes anoxic and, as was implied in Chapter 6, a hostile environment for most higher aqueous life develops. It is the prospect of this situation occurring that has perturbed people about the role of various forms of phosphorus used by the homemaker.

The source of additional phosphate is mainly municipal sewage, partly supplied by human waste and partly (perhaps as much as half) resulting from the use of phosphate-rich detergents. Streams that drain artificially

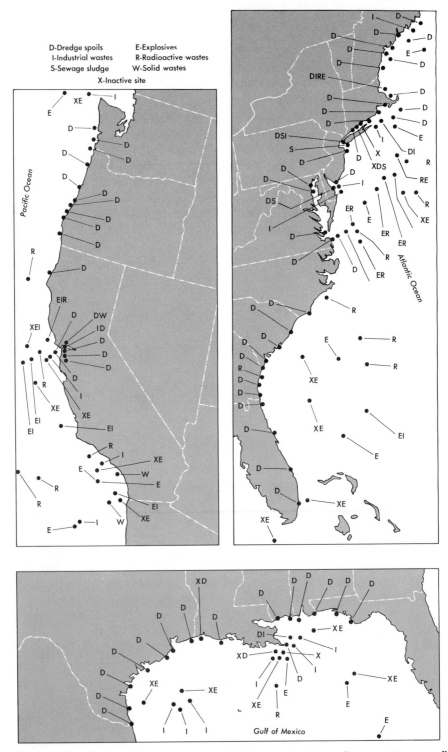

FIGURE 8-1 *Known dumping sites off U.S. coasts. From* "Ocean Dumping," *1970, Council on Environmental Quality.*

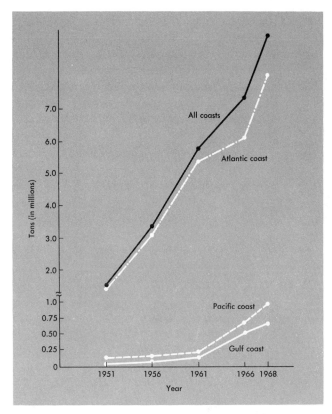

FIGURE 8-2 *Average annual tonnage of waste, exclusive of dredge spoils and explosives, disposed into the sea. From* "Ocean Dumping," *1970, Council on Environmental Quality.*

Table 8–4

The Phosphate in U.S. Runoff*

	Metric Tons Phosphate
Municipal raw sewage	262,000
Urban runoff	100,000
Rural runoff	74,000

Up to 30 percent of the phosphate is ascribable to detergents. The fertilizer and animal phosphate contribution is small compared to man's burden.

*After SCEP, 1970, *Man's Impact on the Global Environment*, MIT Press, Cambridge.

fertilized agricultural land may also carry some excess phosphate, but this point is still to be firmly established. For the United States as a whole, the contribution of municipal wastes to the total supply of phosphorus to the oceans predominates over all other sources (Table 8–4).

The supply of phosphate to lakes and small streams may influence the ecology of those fresh water systems and ultimately result in eutrophication. However, it has been shown that the limiting nutrient for growth of phytoplankton in coastal waters is not phosphorus but nitrogen (Fig. 8–3).

FIGURE 8-3 *Growth of a diatom* (Skeletonema costatum) *in unenriched, ammonium-enriched, and phosphate-enriched water from the New York bight collected from the station shown on the map. After J. H. Ryther and W. M. Durston, 1971, Science, v. 171, pp. 1008–1013.*

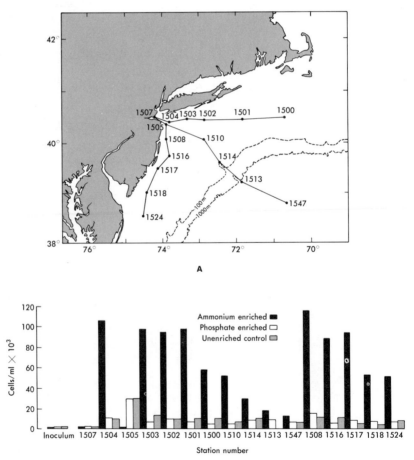

A

B

Thus the increase in the phosphorus supply to the oceans will have very little effect on it. Despite this fact, pressure to diminish the phosphorus burden of municipal waters exists and searches for alternatives continue.

The role of phosphorus in a detergent is to "soften" the water by tying up the ever-present calcium, which inhibits the attack of greases by the alkaline aspect of the detergent. Substitute organic compounds that are strong "chelaters" for metals, including calcium, have been developed. Chelaters tie up a metal by forming a strong chemical bond, thus effectively removing the chelated metal from additional chemical action but still keeping it in solution. The calcium thus tied up cannot inhibit the grease-destruction process. One such compound suggested as a replacement was NTA (nitrotetraacetic acid) but was banned after its hazards became known. A major concern was the discovery that the intermediate degradation products of NTA may be carcinogenic (cancer causing) in large doses. In addition, NTA as a nitrogen-bearing compound, can contribute to the problem of marine eutrophication. Since productivity in coastal waters is apparently limited by nitrogen rather than phosphate, a switch to the nitrogen-bearing compounds would actually have increased the possibility of eutrophication!

Mercury and Other Potentially Toxic Elements

Toxic chemicals and heavy metals from industry are being injected into streams and coastal waters. Included are industrial acids, toxic organic compounds, and such heavy metals as mercury, lead, copper, silver, zinc, cadmium, vanadium, nickel, iron, and manganese. Although other metals are also dumped locally, those just mentioned are found almost everywhere as potential pollutants. The fate of these elements, once they reach the sea, is not completely known, but they can be dangerous to living systems under certain acute conditions. Human poisoning from mercury dumped in the sea has been well documented, but little information is available on the effects of other elements introduced into the oceans.

The case for mercury pollution in coastal waters and its detrimental effect on humans is all too well established as a result of the events at Minamata Bay in Japan (Fig. 8–4). In 1956 a curious set of symptoms indicative of severe toxification of the central nervous system was described at Minamata (Fig. 8–5) and was shown to be of epidemic proportion in that Japanese coastal fishing region. Individual cases having the same syndrome were recognized from the medical records to have been present in some patients as early as 1953. It was discovered that the patients afflicted with the disease were all fishermen and their families, who regularly ate fish caught in Minamata Bay. The disease was marked initially by numbness of the limbs and the lips and soon thereafter by the development of ataxia—

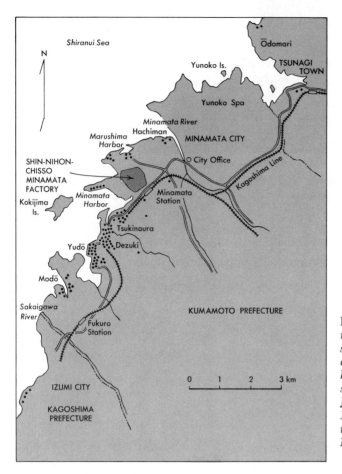

FIGURE 8-4 *Map of Mina-mata Bay region, Japan, showing the distribution of patients (black dots) having symptoms de-scribed in Figure 8-5. After J. Ui and S. Kitamura, 1969, in contribution to the 4th Colloquium for Medical Oceanography, Naples.*

FIGURE 8-5 *The percent of patients having each of the common symptoms as-sociated with the "Mina-mata Bay Syndrome." Af-ter J. Ui and S. Kitamura, 1969, in contribution to the 4th Colloquium for Medical Oceanography, Naples.*

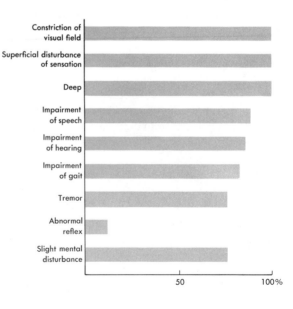

Pollution of the oceans

concentric constriction of the visual field—the most diagnostic symptom of the disease. As the damage increases in severity, coordination deteriorates until unconsciousness and involuntary movements occur. The next step is death.

Of the 116 reported cases of "Minamata Bay Disease" since 1956, 43 have died from it and the physical wastage among the survivors is hideous. The cause of the disease is the excessive ingestion of fish heavily contaminated with a simple organic compound of mercury, dimethyl mercury.

Carefully scientific detective work showed that a chemical plant on Minamata Bay, which produced some basic chemicals used in the plastics industry, was using mercury salts for catalysts. For example, in the production of acetaldehyde ($H_3C - HC = O$) from acetylene ($HC \equiv CH$) mercurous sulfate (Hg_2SO_4) was used as the catalyst.

As a result, small amounts of methyl mercury ions ($Hg(CH_3)^+$) were being released through the waste outfall pipes into Minamata Bay. Methyl mercury then entered shellfish and fish through the food chain, concentrating at each level. When the fishermen caught and ate the polluted fish in the Bay, their bodies in turn began to store the mercury as dimethyl mercury ($Hg(CH_3)_2$) until it reached toxic levels (Fig. 8–6). The length of time between exposure to the highly polluted diet and the appearance of recognizable symptoms was usually 9 months.

Mercury is used in many other industrial processes. The most important is in the manufacture of caustic soda from salt (see Chapter 5). In whatever form it is introduced to sediments, even as metal, it can be mobilized by bacteria by the formation of methyl mercury. Thus, in principle, any mercury deposited in the estuarine zone is subject to release and may thereby increase the concentration level of the surrounding sea water. This process also explains the deep concern regarding the careless dumping of dredge spoils that contain polluted sediments.

It has been found, however, that if the conditions are completely anaerobic in the sediments of the marine environment, the mercury is tightly held in the sediment as the sulfide (HgS) and is not metabolized and released by the bacteria. Indeed, there is a danger that if mercury-polluted dredge spoils are dumped on land where easy aeration is possible by ground water and exposure to air, methyl mercury might be formed much more readily. The runoff and ground water in the immediate vicinity of such a dredge pile could be highly toxic.

Although mercury poisoning, such as the Minamata Bay Disease, has been known for a long time (It is believed that Lewis Carroll's "Mad Hatter" characterization is based on the fact that hat makers in England in the nineteenth century gradually ingested enough mercury, used in processing felt, to develop damage to the central nervous system over a period of time.), it has not yet been recognized in other countries in association

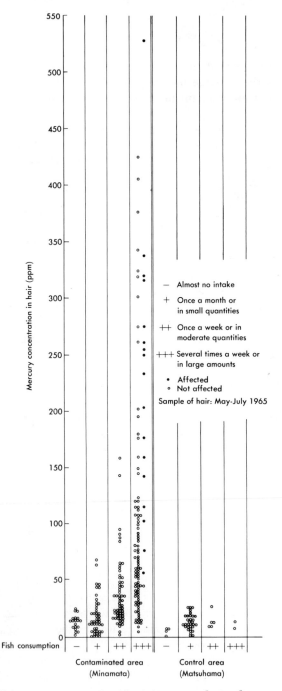

FIGURE 8-6 *The mercury content of hair from people in the contaminated area of Minamata and a noncontaminated area (Matsuhama) in Japan, as related to the frequency of fish eating. Black dots represent patients having the Minamata Bay disease syndrome. After J. Ui and S. Kitamura, 1969, in contribution to the 4th Colloquium for Medical Oceanography, Naples.*

Pollution of the oceans

with the marine environment. The explanation may lie not so much in the absence of mercury pollution in coastal waters and sediments in other parts of the world as in the gastronomic habits of the local people.

It has been demonstrated, for example, that acetaldehyde plants at Ravenna, Italy, on the Adriatic Sea also used a mercury salt as a catalyst and thus were potential mercury polluters, but the general pollution of the region is so great that the local fish taste oily and are not eaten. Moreover, the fishermen are gradually abandoning their trade in favor of tourism. In Sweden mercury pollution has been mainly derived from agricultural chemicals or slimicides used in the wood-pulp industry, and the effects have been mainly felt by birds. The human casualties, if they exist, are not documented.

It is not surprising that concern over mercury pollution, and by extension, pollution of coastal waters by other heavy metals, has aroused the ire of scientists and the public alike. As a result, operations involving metals as waste are being more carefully controlled in the United States.

In addition to the heavy metal pollution of coastal waters, the level of certain highly volatile elements can be expected to increase in the open ocean as the result of atmospheric transport. This situation has been clearly established for lead (Fig. 8-7). The surface water of many parts of the ocean already have higher lead concentrations than deep waters. This is the reverse of the normal case where the deep waters are enriched in trace metals relative to surface waters because of biological transport (Fig. 8-8). The change in concentration is more an indication that there is metal pollution than a point for immediate alarm about danger to marine life. Indeed, we are not certain that an effect is demonstrable at all.

FIGURE 8-7 *The vertical distribution of lead at three stations in the oceans showing contamination in some locales close to intense human activity. After T. Chow and C. Patterson, 1966,* Earth and Planetary Science Letters, *v. 1, pp. 397–400.*

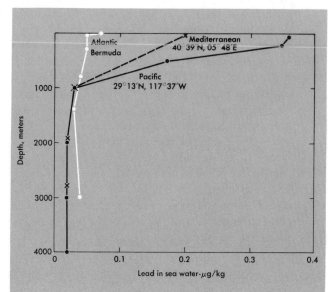

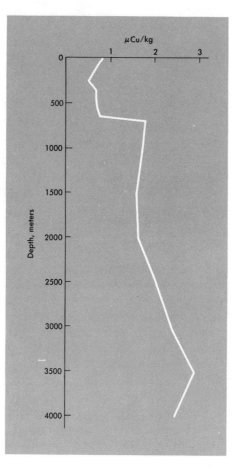

FIGURE 8-8 *The vertical distribution of copper in the East Pacific off the California coast. After D. Spencer et al., 1970, Jour. Geophys. Res., v. 75, pp. 7688–7696.*

The one commonly used heavy metal that is easily volatilized is mercury, and it is to be expected that it should be found concentrated in ocean surface waters. The available data, although sparse, indicate that there is no significant difference between surface and deep waters in either the Atlantic or Pacific oceans. The reason probably is that the volcanic supply of mercury far exceeds the amount volatilized by human activity. This situation suggests that there should not be any increase in mercury concentration in fish living in the open ocean far from polluted coastal sites. The high levels of mercury in swordfish and, to a lesser extent, in tuna have nothing to do with the potential coastal mercury-pollution problem. These levels are due to the fact that the mercury concentration, as with some other metals, is enhanced in these large predators as the result of the eating of smaller fish. Their mercury concentrations seem to be normal, a fact that has been clearly shown by the analysis of swordfish and tuna canned or preserved in museums since the turn of the century compared to analyses of contemporary swordfish and tuna. No increase in mercury concentrations with time was found.

Perhaps there is an important lesson for us in these discoveries. The required detective work had not been completed prior to the ban on swordfish. Hence the decision was based on little evidence, and, consequently, a productive fishery has been all but eliminated. In our haste to condemn by extrapolating from a narrow specific case, we have caused a net decrease in the well-being of hundreds of fishermen. We have also deprived the consumer of a desirable product that we now know can be eaten without worry, provided we do not do it to excess. Because so many foods can be prescribed with this precaution, it appears that our mercury-in-swordfish hysteria may have needlessly deprived us of a legitimate human pleasure.

Petroleum

One of the most widespread oceanic pollutants is petroleum and its distilled products. Indeed, a metaphor often used in the past, "pouring oil on troubled waters," is rarely heard any longer, vividly indicating by its absence the degree to which we now think that oil on water is more of a liability than an asset.

In the coastal waters, petroleum or its refined products may be released to the sea from any of several sources: natural seepage from geological oil deposits; accidental loss from offshore drilling operations; accidents and sloppy handling during loading and unloading of the oil; collisions and wrecks resulting in cargo loss; sea water flushing of oil tankers at sea; and the atmospheric transport of the more volatile components of petroleum or its refined products. In addition, used lubricating oils for which there is neither a market nor a clearly identifiable scheme for disposal may make their way to the sea in coastal cities.

The magnitude of the problem of oil pollution at sea can be seen in the following statistics. In 1969 the total worldwide production of crude oil was 1820 million metric tons. Of this amount, it is estimated that 1180 million metric tons were transported by oil tankers. Assessments of the loss of oil to the marine environment show that it happens mainly in the coastal zone and that it ranges from a low of one million metric tons to an upper limit of about 10 million metric tons each year. Thus it is possible that up to about 0.5 percent of the oil produced is released to the environment directly—and most of this in the coastal zone.

The acute local releases of oil on a large scale, such as the *Torrey Canyon* incident near Lands End, England, in 1967, the Santa Barbara oil well blowout and leakage in California in 1969, and the Gulf of Mexico blowouts, have immediate and direct effects on organisms, some of which appear to be irreversible. Sometimes the attempted corrective measures, such as bombing and applying detergent for the inactivation of the oil, as in the case of the *Torrey Canyon* incident, have been more catastrophic than the

Table 8–5

The Organic Molecules Making Up Petroleum

Class of Compounds	Examples

1. Relatively stable paraffin series of straight molecular chain compounds with the general formula C_nH_{2n+2}. The series is sometimes called the alkanes, and methane, CH_4, is its commonest member.

2. Relatively stable cycloparaffin series of molecular-ring structure compounds with the general formual C_nH_{2n}. The series is sometimes called the napthenes, and cyclopentane, C_5H_{10}, and cyclohexane, C_6H_{12}, are the two most common compounds.

3. Relatively unstable molecular-ring structure group with the general formula C_nH_{2n-6}, of which benzene, C_6H_6, is the most common compound.

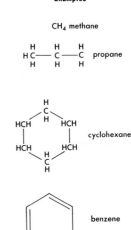

actual spill itself. The small continuous leakages and their growing burden on the marine environment are more difficult to assess, but in the long run they may have important consequences for the alteration of the living assemblage, at least in local marine environments. Unlike mercury, however, oil pollution has produced no reports of direct physical harm to humans. Many of the compounds comprising oil (Table 8–5) are known to be cancer producers in a number of organisms if present in high enough concentrations. In addition, direct and physiologic effects on fin fish, shellfish, and some microorganisms engulfed by an oil spill will result in the virtual destruction of the marine biological community. However, if the oil is finely dispersed in the form of an emulsion, bacteria will begin to attack the oil as a food source. The limiting factors controlling the speed and efficiency of the process are temperature, nutrient element (such as nitrogen) supply, and the size of the organic globules. Under ideal conditions, the rate of oxidation of oil by bacteria in the ocean may be between 36 to 350 grams per cubic meter per year.

In Arctic regions the speed of bacterial destruction of oil is much slower than this rate. If the degradation rate is attenuated, either from low temperature or from the absence of sufficient nitrogen or phosphorus, the oil globules will coalesce and form large tarry balls because of the loss of the light molecular-weight components by evaporation or solution. Once these "tar" balls are formed, they are virtually indestructable. Such tar balls have been found on almost every coastline of the world.

Petroleum dumped into the open ocean may be less efficiently destroyed by bacteria because of the generally lower nutrient concentration found in the central parts of ocean basins compared to the margins. Clumps of tarry material have clogged scientific plankton tow nets for years. In 1969 Thor Heyerdahl reported on the almost continuous sea of debris, dominated by tarry lumps, observed during the slow voyage across the tropical Atlantic on the *Ra*.

It is hard to evaluate the degree of harm, other than aesthetic disruptions, of oil in the open seas. Clearly, if the rate of dumping exceeds the rate of its destruction by bacteria, oil will eventually be a serious factor in limiting plankton productivity by limiting the total area of utility. Oil pollution in the open sea may also enhance the biological uptake of chlorinated hydrocarbons by localizing these compounds in ingestible globules.

Oil spills at sea could perhaps be controlled if a supply of nutrient and an appropriate mixture of destructive bacteria were dumped on the site of the spill, but these emergency measures may be the least-satisfactory way to treat the problem. A better method is clearly to diminish the amount of petroleum released into the sea, for much of it is not of accidental origin. It is hard to imagine what remedial steps could be taken if one of the 500,000 dead weight ton "super tankers," which are dominating the field of oil transportation, broke up or lost its cargo at sea. Almost a half million tons of oil could be spilled, and the oil slick might eventually cover hundreds of square miles. The destruction of marine life at the site of the spill would be massive, and if the oil persists for long periods of time, it will eventually affect the quality of coastal waters adjacent to the spill site.

Chlorinated Hydrocarbons

The worldwide distribution of chlorinated hydrocarbon, such as DDT and PCB, has been well documented by the popular press in the United States. DDT, for example, is sprayed over land and some coastal areas to control insects. This spraying is done both to protect agricultural crops and to destroy disease carriers. Its successes have been dramatic and, in some fashion, have affected almost all of mankind. For example, from the beginning of its use near the end of World War II, DDT has virtually eliminated malaria in the U.S.S.R., where it was of endemic proportions in certain areas. Its use for controlling the malaria-carrying mosquito still contributes to the well-being of millions of people in India and in Africa and annually saves the lives of hundreds of thousands.

It is not surprising, then, that for many people in the world DDT enjoys the same respect as antibiotics do for the Western countries. Since most of the Western countries fall in temperate climatic zones and have not been afflicted with endemic malaria, nor with continually threatened agricultural crops, the major focus on DDT has shifted from its many good effects to the harm it has done, or is potentially capable of doing, when injected into the natural system. The reason for this growing concern is based on experience. There is no question that certain degradation products of DDT, when metabolized by animals, can result in the distortion of some of their natural functions. Birds are a notable example. Certain species of birds have been endangered because the rising DDT concentration in their diets results in a deterioration of their eggshells, and eventually in sterility, so that survival of their species is now in danger.

If DDT were easily destroyed by natural chemical processes, the concern about it would be less intense. Unfortunately, it is a well-known property of chlorinated hydrocarbons that they are extremely resistant to degradation and thus persist for long periods of time. DDT ingested by animals is stored in the fatty parts of the animal and is thus transmitted up the food chain with increasing concentration each time an animal higher in the chain consumes one lower in it.

The combination of all these factors affecting DDT—its proven toxicity to animals, its extensive atmospheric and consequent oceanic mobility, its persistence and its magnification up the food chain—indeed make DDT and the related chlorinated hydrocarbons of serious concern to mankind. As a consequence the United States has severely restricted the use of DDT within its national boundaries.

DDT is not found at the very start of the food chain—the phytoplankton. Therefore it must enter the food chain as particles independent of the phytoplankton. The fact that DDT is virtually insoluble in water but fairly soluble in fats and oils suggests that it is sequestered in oil globules at the ocean surface and that it enters the food chain by animals ingesting the tiny globules. The increasing DDT supply to the oceans is now reflected in the increasing concentrations found in marine organisms. Although this situation provides a strong argument for curtailing its use, the disadvantages must be weighed against the needs of underdeveloped countries, particularly in Asia and Africa, where hunger and malaria are still overwhelming problems. Who can argue with conviction that the lives of millions of people already on the Earth are expendable in order to ward off a future potential danger to marine life and the future human users of it? For this reason, the World Health Organization has supported the continued use of DDT in underdeveloped countries.

The other class of chlorinated hydrocarbons that has come to public attention as environmental hazards are the group of compounds called polychlorinated biphenyls (PCB). The main use of PCB is in heat-transfer systems, such as transformers, although this class of compounds has also been used as plasticizers and in many other ways. Like DDT, it has a very long residence time and thus the danger from PCB is growing. Human deaths from the use of oils for cooking that were heavily contaminated with PCB have already been reported in Japan. Startlingly, the level of PCB in certain marine organisms has been found to be greater than that in the poisoned humans. This fact indicates that PCB, like DDT, is long lived and is magnified through the food chain. Although the uses of PCB are diverse, the group of compounds does not appear to have the redeeming qualities of DDT with regard to disease control and agriculture. Thus there is a growing concern for the indiscriminant dumping of PCB into the environment. It may, in a very real sense, be a more destructive pollutant than DDT.

Suggestions for further reading

Chapter 2
The oceanic realm

M. G. Gross, *Oceanography*. Englewood Cliffs, N.J.: Prentice-Hall, 1972.

K. K. Turekian, *Oceans*. Englewood Cliffs, N.J.: Prentice-Hall, 1968.

Chapter 3
The resource concept

B. J. Skinner, *Earth Resources*. Englewood Cliffs, N.J.: Prentice-Hall, 1969.

The Staff, *Mineral Facts and Figures*. Bull. 630, U.S. Bureau of Mines, 1965.

Chapter 4
Mineral resources of the seabed

J. L. Mero, *The Mineral Resources of the Sea*. Amsterdam: Elsevier, 1965.

Mineral Resources of the Sea. United Nations Report E/4973, 26 April, 1971.

Chapter 5
Energy

T. J. Gray and O. K. Gashus (eds.), *Tidal Power*. New York: Plenum Press, 1972.

M. K. Hubbert, "Energy Resources," *Resources and Man*. The Committee on Resources and Man, Nat. Acad. Sci., San Francisco: W. H. Freeman and Co., 1969.

Committee on Petroleum Resources under the Ocean Floor, *Petroleum Resources under the Ocean Floor*. Washington, D.C.: National Petroleum Council, 1625 "K" Street N.W., 20006, 1969.

Chapter 6
The chemical resources of sea water

J. P. Riley and R. Chester, *Introduction to Marine Chemistry*. London: Academic Press, 1971.

Chapter 7
Desalination

S. N. Levine (ed.), *Selected Papers on Desalination and Ocean Technology*. New York: Daven Publications, 1968.

P. Sporn, *Fresh Waters from Saline Waters*. Oxford: Pergamon Press, 1966.

Chapter 8
Pollution of the oceans

D. W. Hood (ed.), *Impingement of Man on the Oceans*. New York: John Wiley and Sons, 1971.

Index

Petroleum (*cont.*)
    subsea resources, 77–83
Philippine Islands, 10
Phosphate, 26 ,40, 129–133
Phosphorite, 31, 40, 46–48
Phosphorus, 18, 19, 94, 97,
    120, 129, 132–133,
    140
Photosynthesis, 19, 24, 74
Phytoplankton, 19, 129, 132,
    142
Pipelines, transport of water
    by, 121–122
Plaster, 55
Plate tectonics, 12–14, 41,
    57–62, 80
Platinum, 31, 32, 50, 58, 95
Pleistocene Epoch, 53
Pliny the Elder, 4
Pliocene Epoch, 76
Pollution
    air, 70
    of oceans, 26, 124–143
        atmospheric transport,
            124–127, 137, 139
        bulk material dumping,
            127–129
        chlorinated hydrocar-
            bons, 141–143
        coastal zone, 124–125
        mercury, 133–139
        petroleum, 139–141
        phosphate and eutrophi-
            cation, 129–133
        shipping and, 125
Polonium, 95
Polychlorinated biphenyls
    (PCB), 141–143
Population growth, 69, 71
Potash, 31
Potassium, 40, 41, 94, 102
Potassium salts, 46
Potential resources, 26, 36,
    54, 60–61
Power Systems Company, 90
Praseodymium, 95
Pressure, of sea water, 15–16
Promethium, 95
Propane, 117
Protactinium, 95
Protein, sources of, 26–27

Quartz, 49, 53

Ra, 141
Radium, 95
Radon, 95
Rainfall, 72, 118, 125
Rance Estuary, 85, 86, 88
Ravenna, Italy, mercury
    pollution, 137
Recycling, 26
Red Sea, 59–61
Renewable resources, 24–28
Resources

depleting, 25–26
natural, 24
potential, 26, 36, 54,
    60–61
renewable, 24–28
See also Chemical re-
    sources of sea water;
    Mineral resources
Reverse osmosis, as method
    of desalination,
    115–116
Rhenium, 95
Rhine River, 4
Rhodium, 95
Rhone delta, 9
Rivers, 2, 21, 23
Romanche Trench, 58
Romania, 71
Ross shelf, 121
Rubidium, 94
Ruby, 50
Ruthenium, 95
Rutile, 50, 52, 53, 54

Sacramento River, 122–123
St. Paul's Rock, 11
Salinity, 14–16, 21, 110
Salt, 31, 40, 41, 102–107
Salt domes, 40–46
Salton Sea, 61
Samarium, 95
San Francisco Bay, 103–104,
    122–123
Sand, 30, 31, 49, 55, 56
Santa Barbara, California,
    139
Sapphire, 50
Sargasso Sea, 125
Scandium, 94
Scheldt River, 4
Sea ice, 120
Sea level, 21–23
Sea water, 14–20
    chemical resources,
        92–108
        bromine, 107–108
        magnesium, 105–107
        sodium chloride,
            102–107
        trace-element concen-
            trations, 92–102
    evaporation sequence, 24,
        41, 103–104, 109–110
    pressure, 15
    salinity, 14–16
    temperature, 15
    See also Desalination;
        Oceans
Seabed, *see* Ocean basins
Sediments, 6, 9–12, 37–42,
    52, 59–63, 75–82, 97–
    99, 105, 135
Selenium, 94
Sewage sludge, 127
Shelf break, 8–9

Shelf ice, 120–121
Shells, 54, 56
Shipping, pollution and, 125
Shrimp, 28
Sierra Nevada Mountains,
    118
Sigsbee Knolls, 81
Silicon, 18, 19, 94
Silver, 31, 95, 98, 99, 100,
    133
Sodium, 94
Sodium chloride, 41,
    102–107
Solar energy, 72–74
Solar salt, 41, 103, 104
Solid waste, 127
Springs, 23
Steam engine, invention of,
    70
Steel, 31
Still, as method of desalina-
    tion, 110
Stone, 55
Stratification of oceans,
    15–16
Streams, 20, 132
Strontium, 94
Sudbury, Ontario, 58
Sulfide, 44
Sulfur, 31, 40, 42–46, 94,
    107
Sumatra, 79
Sun
    evaporation sequence, 24,
        41, 103–104, 109–110
    hydrogen fusion, 91
    hydrologic cycle and, 20
    solar energy, 72–74
    tidal cycles, 83–84
Superphosphate, 47
Sweden, mercury pollution,
    137
Swordfish, mercury levels in,
    138–139
Sylvite, 46

Tantalum, 95
Technetium, 95
Tellurium, 95
Temperature, of sea water,
    16–16
Tennessee, phosphorite
    deposits in, 48
Teribium, 95
Tetraethyl lead, 107
Texas, building materials in,
    56
Thailand, 52
Thallium, 95
Thermal energy, 73, 83,
    88–89
Thermocline, 16
Thermohaline circulation, 18
Thorium, 93, 95
Thulium, 95